THE ART & DESIGN SERIES

For beginners, students, and working professionals in both fine and commercial arts, these books offer practical how-to introductions to a variety of areas in contemporary art and design.

Each illustrated volume is written by a working artist, a specialist in his or her field, and each concentrates on an individual area—from advertising layout or printmaking to interior design, painting, and cartooning, among others. Each contains information that artists will find useful in the studio, in the classroom, and in the marketplace.

BOOKS IN THE SERIES:

Carving Wood and Stone: An Illustrated Manual
ARNOLD PRINCE

Chinese Painting in Four Seasons:
A Manual of Aesthetics & Techniques
LESLIE TSENG –TSENG YU/text with Gail Schiller Tuchman

The Complete Book of Cartooning
JOHN ADKINS RICHARDSON

Creating an Interior
HELENE LEVENSON, A.S.I.D.

Drawing: The Creative Process
SEYMOUR SIMMONS III and MARC S.A. WINER

Drawing with Pastels
RON LISTER

Graphic Illustration: Tools & Techniques
for Beginning Illustrators
MARTA THOMA

How to Sell Your Artwork: A Complete Guide
for Commercial and Fine Artists
MILTON K. BERLYE

Ideas for Woodturning
ANDERS THORLIN

The Language of Layout
BUD DONAHUE

Lithography: A Complete Guide
MARY ANN WENNIGER

Nature Drawing: A Tool for Learning
CLARE WALKER LESLIE

Nature Photography: A Guide to
Better Outdoor Pictures
STAN OSOLINSKI

Painting and Drawing: Discovering Your
Own Visual Language
ANTHONY TONEY

Photographic Lighting: Learning to See
RALPH HATTERSLEY

Photographic Printing
RALPH HATTERSLEY

Photographing Nudes
CHARLES HAMILTON

A Practical Guide for Beginning Painters
THOMAS GRIFFITH

Printmaking: A Beginning Handbook
WILLIAM C. MAXWELL/photos by Howard Unger

Silkscreening
MARIA TERMINI

Silver: An Instructional Guide
to the Silversmith's Art
RUEL O. REDINGER

Teaching Children to Draw:
A Guide for Teachers and Parents
MARJORIE WILSON and BRENT WILSON

Transparent Watercolor:
Painting Methods and Materials
INESSA DERKATSCH

Understanding Paintings:
The Elements of Composition
FREDERICK MALINS

Woodturning for Pleasure
GORDON STOKES/revised by Robert Lento

MARTA THOMA
is a free-lance illustrator
and has taught graphic illustration
at the University of California–Berkeley.

A SPECTRUM BOOK

Prentice-Hall, Inc.
Englewood Cliffs, New Jersey 07632

Marta
Thoma

Graphic
Illustration

Tools &
Techniques
for
Beginning
Illustrators

Library of Congress Cataloging in Publication Data

Thoma, Marta.
   Graphic illustration.

   "A Spectrum Book."
   Bibliography: p.
   Includes index.
   1. Graphic arts—Technique.   2. Artists'
tools.   I. Title.
NC1000.T5   741.6   82-3739
ISBN 0-13-363374-8   AACR2
ISBN 0-13-363366-7 (pbk.)

THE ART & DESIGN SERIES

Editorial/production supervision by Heath Lynn Silberfeld
    and Cyndy Lyle Rymer
Interior and color insert design by Christine Gehring-Wolf
Cover design by Jeannette Jacobs
Cover and title page illustration by Marta Thoma
Page layout by Diane Heckler-Koromhas

A SPECTRUM BOOK

Printed in the United States of America

ISBN 0-13-363374-8

ISBN 0-13-363366-7 (PBK.)

This Spectrum Book is available to businesses and organizations
at a special discount when ordered in large quantities. For
information, contact Prentice-Hall, Inc., General Book Division,
Special Sales, Englewood Cliffs, N.J. 07632.

Prentice-Hall International, Inc., *London*
Prentice-Hall of Australia Pty. Limited, *Sydney*
Prentice-Hall Canada, Inc., *Toronto*
Prentice-Hall of India Private Limited, *New Delhi*
Prentice-Hall of Japan, Inc., *Tokyo*
Prentice-Hall of Southeast Asia Pte. Ltd., *Singapore*
Whitehall Books Limited, *Wellington, New Zealand*

Contents

Preface   xi

Introduction:
The History
of Illustration   1

An Ancient Art Form   2
Illustration Since 1900   3
Current Trends   6

Chapter
one

Basic Techniques   9

Getting to Know the Assignment   10
The Thumbnail Sketch   11
The Rough Drawing   18
Photography as a Tool   24
The Role of the Designer   29
Suggested Exercises   31

Chapter
two
The Simple
Line Drawing &
Variations   33

Materials   35
Method #1   35
Method #2   35
Variations on the
Simple Line Drawing   36
Suggested Exercises   48

Chapter
three
More
Illustration
Techniques 51

Ink Wash 52
Watercolors 54
Color Theory 59
Suggested Exercises 65
Colored Inks 65
Painting with Gouache 67
Colored Pencils 67
Acrylic Paints 71
Oil Paints 75
Suggested Exercises 77
The Airbrushed Illustration 78
Suggested Exercises 87
Color Separations 87
Taking Care of Your
Finished Illustration 94

Chapter
four
Communicating
Your Ideas 97

Cultural Images & Content Symbols 99
The Relationship of Images 100
Gestures & Attitudes of Images 102
Abstract Symbolism 107
Communication Checklist 108
Suggested Exercises 108
Drawing to Communicate 108
Suggested Exercises 108
Drawing Difficult Subjects 109

Chapter five
Special Subjects 117

Fantasy & Surrealism 118
Suggested Exercises 127
People & Portraits 127
Suggested Exercises 138
Product Illustration 138
Suggested Exercises 144
Fashion Illustration 144
Suggested Exercises 147
Children's Book Illustration 148
Suggested Exercises 150
Technical Illustration 151
Suggested Exercises 153
Medical Illustration 154
Architectural & Mechanical
Illustration 155

Chapter six
Illustration as a Profession 159

Preparing a Portfolio 160
Finding Your Clients 161
Promoting Yourself 162
Finding Your Style 163

Glossary 165

Bibliography 169

History of Illustration 169
Illustration Subjects 169
General Skills 170

Index 171

Dedication & Acknowledgments

This book is dedicated to Michael Hodges.

I wish to extend special thanks to Elsa Hildabrand for typing the manuscript and making helpful suggestions.

I would like to thank the artists whose illustrations are included in this book. I am especially grateful to those who shared their thoughts with me on subjects from art techniques to more philosophical ideas about art.

I would also like to thank the following people who have been helpful along the way: Judy Olson, Carol Thompson, Chris Blum, Kerig Pope, Paul Pratchenko, Ed Wong-Ligda, John Ihle, Robert Bechtle, and Paolo Carosone.

Preface

I am happy to be able to write a book that provides beginners with a vast amount of information about the illustration profession. If I had been able to find a book like this when I was beginning as an artist—which was not too long ago—I could have avoided learning some of these things, as they say, the hard way.

I had two major goals while writing this book. First, I tried to take the mystery out of the process of making an illustration. Each step of planning and making an illustration is explained from beginning to end. Contemporary illustrating techniques are described in detail, as are the communication, composition, and drawing techniques used to develop the concept of an illustration. I have also included such professional shortcuts as transfer methods and the use of photography.

My other goal was to inspire the reader to be as creative as possible. A textbook on art must tread a fine line, offering advice and information without saying "this is how it is done" and "this is what it should look like." The exercises throughout the book should help the reader become more skillful and, at the same time, encourage self-expression.

I studied fine art for several years before I became an illustrator and received a B.A. in fine art from the University of California at Berkeley, and later an M.A. from San Francisco State University. In

graduate school I planned, like many of my fellow grad students, to complete my studies and find work as a full-time professor immediately, which would enable me to teach art and have plenty of spare time for my own artwork. I assumed that teaching would provide most of my income.

The idea of teaching was a natural for me. I come from a long line of teachers. Both of my grandmothers taught, one of them in a one-room schoolhouse. My mother and father both earned Ph.D.s and taught at universities, and my three older sisters earn a living by teaching. The love and high regard for teaching passed down to me gave me the patience to write this book and enjoy it as much as I did.

However, I did not find a job waiting after graduation, and while I was looking, I discovered that I could make a living as an illustrator. Along the way, I had to learn the technical aspects of illustrating by doing and by receiving helpful advice from those who employed me. The result was that I discovered I loved illustrating.

I found the field to be satisfying because it challenges me to stretch my imagination and improve my skills every day. In addition, it is rewarding to be well paid for skills I have worked long and hard to develop. And what could be more fun than making a living drawing pictures?

How to Use This Book

This book is designed to be used on a number of levels—by the beginner and the more advanced student, alone or in class. How you use it will depend on your situation and experience.

FOR THE BEGINNER

Little or no art-class experience classifies you as a beginner. If this is the first time you have tried to learn to draw, take heart. With the beginner in mind, the reader will be guided step by step through the process of making an illustration, right from the beginning. Plunge in, study the information, and try the exercises that will get your hand moving. Here are some suggestions especially for the beginner.

1. Concentrate on the first two chapters until those basic skills are ingrained. These chapters teach the fundamental illustrating skills used in all of the chapters that follow.
2. Study the sections on composition, design, and color theory carefully. They will give you the essentials of design and color courses in a nutshell.
3. Do the exercises that are listed at the end of each chapter. This is especially important if you are working independently since it will help you to discipline yourself. The exercises are written to help you learn the concept in the chapter, and they are meant to be fun, as well as instructive.
4. Study the sections on photography carefully. They will show you how to use photos and tracing techniques as aids in drawing.

While drawing skills are an important part of illustrating, it is the results that count and not how the drawing is done. As a beginner with no drawing experience, you can get results by tracing or copying from photographs. Let's say, for example, that an exercise calls for you to draw a car. If you cannot draw a car from memory or from life, trace a car from a photograph. This is not cheating. Some form of tracing or transferring is used by most professionals.

5. As you do the exercises, you will accumulate several finished illustrations. Take care of them so that you can use the best ones in a portfolio later. Beginners have a tendency to toss a drawing in a drawer or some other place where it is sure to get soiled or crumpled. Make it a point to preserve your finished illustrations from the very beginning.
6. As your confidence grows, progress to trying more challenging techniques. How much you learn and how advanced you become are up to you.

FOR THE READER WITH DESIGN AND DRAWING EXPERIENCE

Whether self-taught or formally trained, every experienced student should start at the beginning of the book and work to the end. The more advanced students will learn the early material quickly and go on to more challenging techniques. However, if you have had only one or two art courses, it is best to follow the instructions for beginners, taking each new section a step at a time. Beginner suggestions 3, 4, 5, and 6 contain good tips for you.

There are several advantages to be gained from the orderly progression. Proceeding from beginning to end and completing the suggested exercises will lead you to accumulate illustrations to put into a portfolio. The early chapters should not be skipped, because a portfolio should include samples of black-and-white artwork and possibly some line illustrations. Of course, you will want to include color artwork from exercises in the later chapters as well.

In addition, you will find in this book many challenging techniques to try, including airbrushing and collage, and you will find interesting professional artists' descriptions of their work and the techniques they use, some of which are unique and experimental.

IN THE CLASSROOM

This book can be used as a text for beginning, intermediate, and advanced students. It guides the student through progressively more challenging techniques and communication concepts and covers more than one semester's worth of material.

How fast students progress through the book will depend on the prerequisites for the course. The teacher can use it as a curriculum guide or can use separate sections selectively to suit his or her style of teaching and the needs of the class.

'The sail hurled away both knight and horse along with it.'

Introduction:
The History
of Illustration

Painting and illustration developed along similar paths through history, being, in many respects, one and the same. Both have traditionally been tied to literary sources of inspiration such as the Bible, but paintings were made to adorn walls and ceilings, while illustrations were made to adorn manuscripts, to help tell a story or record an event. Both paintings and illustrations were originally rare, costly, handmade objects owned only by the very wealthy.

An Ancient Art Form

The first-known illustrations were made in Egypt between 2100 and 1800 BC to illustrate manuscripts written on papyrus in roll form. There is evidence of large-scale workshops for the writing and illustrating of manuscripts whose subjects included astronomy, magic, erotica, and science. One such book was a religious work, *The Book of the Dead*. As the manuscript was written, spaces were left for illustrations to be filled in. The style of the illustrations was similar to Egyptian wall paintings of the period.

The first book as we know it, in "codex" form with leaves bound on one side, was made in the first century AD. Rolls of papyrus continued in use, but manuscript writing in book form slowly became more prevalent. Gradually illustrations came to be placed on a separate page instead of being interspersed with the text. Decorative borders surrounding pages of writing were often included in Byzantine, Celtic, and western European manuscripts.

Sometime during the 700s a method of printing illustrations was invented in China. The earliest dated book with a printed illustration was a Buddhist discourse known as the *Diamond Sutra* which appeared in 868 AD with a woodcut.

Europe would not follow suit until the fifteenth century, at the height of the Renaissance. The early Renaissance had seen many advances in the arts; painters and illustrators alike became interested in creating the illusion of reality, and they learned to use perspective and foreshortened figures to create an illusion of deep space. Illustrators of the time worked to devise a method of reproducing artwork for multiple editions of books, because hiring copyists to hand copy an artist's original illustration for each book proved less than satisfactory, especially in scientific books, where plants and animals lost their original characteristics in the copying process.

The first printed illustrations produced in Europe appeared in the late 1400s in German "block books"—so-called because both the picture and part of the text were engraved and printed together on a single wood block. Ulrich Boner's *Der Edelstein* was printed by this method in 1461 by Albrecht Pfister in Bamberg, Germany. In some of these early printed books, a picture's aesthetic value was more important than its fidelity to the text: in *Nurnberg Chronicle* (1493), the same picture of a town is labeled "Ulm" on one page and "Damascus" on another. Two books of the period that were notable for fine woodcuts were *Dance of Death*, illustrated by Hans Holbein the Younger, and *Ship of Fools*, illustrated by Albrecht Dürer.

To make a woodblock print, a design is drawn on a flat surface of wood and the background is carved away. The design, which stands out in relief, is inked and pressed onto paper, either by hand or with a press. The first press used for this purpose was a screw press.

Intaglio printing is a process in which ink is rubbed into incisions made on a metal or stone plate. The plate is run through a press, which forces the ink lines to print on paper. After it was invented in the fifteenth century, it replaced woodblock engraving because more delicate lines and subtle tonal qualities could be reproduced. The technique was not as convenient as wood engraving because illustrations had to be printed separately from the manuscript. However, the technique was aesthetically pleasing, and it remained popular for about 200 years.

In the early 1800s, Thomas Bewick, an English engraver, developed an improved technique for printing on wood, which made reproductions as fine as metal engravings but employed a simplified printing process that enabled the manuscript to be printed simultaneously. In addition, the invention of lithography at this time permitted artists to paint or draw an illustration instead of having to engrave it.

By 1830, illustrated books were available at comparatively low prices, which enabled the average person to purchase them. *Penny Magazine* was the first periodical to use many illustrations and to aim at popular tastes. Soon other newspapers and magazines began featuring illustrations.

Photographs were first introduced to illustrate books in 1844. Even more important, however, was the development of photographic techniques to replace the hand-printing processes of engraving and lithography. By 1920, photoengraving had completely superseded hand-printing techniques in magazine, newspaper, and book publishing.

While hand engraving was becoming obsolete in the nineteenth century, some artists rebelled against what they considered the loss of a fine art. William Morris and Maurice Denis led a movement to revitalize other artists' enthusiasm for the art of printmaking, and several books printed at this time featured hand-printed illustrations. These books, like other pieces of fine art, sold for very high prices. The enthusiasm for sharing the art of hand printing has lasted through this century, and most colleges and universities offer a fine-arts degree in printmaking, which includes the study of etching, engraving, woodblock printing, and lithography.

Illustration Since 1900

Illustration as an art form changed radically in the twentieth century as photoengraving replaced the older crafts of hand engraving and hand-printed lithography. With the new photographic process, any painting, drawing, sculpture, or other medium that could be photographed could be used to make an illustration. Today, illustrations are made in every medium that is used for the visual

2

2 Artist: Winslow Homer
Title: *Gathering Berries*
Client: *Harper's Weekly,*
1874

3 Artist: Aubrey Beardsley
Title: *The Peacock Skirt*
Media: Pen-and-ink
Courtesy of the Fogg Art
Museum, Harvard Univer-
sity Bequest—Grenville L.
Winthrop.

arts, including three-dimentional media such as collage, embroidery, found-object sculpture, and paper sculpture.
Gallery painting techniques are still used for illustration, just as they were hundreds of years ago. But since illustration emerged as a popular art form in the 1800s, it has from time to time veered from the course of fine art trends in response to a much larger audience, a hodgepodge of wealthy and poor, educated and uneducated people.

Illustrations have traditionally been decorative or representational, since these qualities are highly regarded by the general population. Decorative or

well-designed art makes a page pleasing and interesting, while representational art invites viewers to identify their own feelings and experiences with those represented on the page. Representational art can also be informative and instructive.

When representational art has been in style, illustrative art has been embraced. The art movements of impressionism, expressionism, and cubism were representational, while being very inventive and expressive. In the early 1900s, artists such as Toulouse-Lautrec, Aubrey Beardsley, and Pablo Picasso created artistic posters and book illustrations.

Beginning in the 1930s, painting became progressively abstract, and a new movement, abstract expressionism, dominated the years 1940–1965. Representational imagery was discarded altogether, along with other traditional ideas of painting, in what may have been a reaction to the development of photography, which replaced painting as a means of recording nature, events, and people realistically.

After abstract expressionism peaked as a new trend, minimal art emerged in the late 1960s and 1970s. Artists of the minimal school attempted to eliminate as much as possible from a painting, including color, design, and support materials. A painting in this style may be a large canvas painted entirely gray.

During these years, illustrators remained responsive to the larger population, who for the most part rejected abstract expressionism and minimal art as "emperor's new clothes" phenomena. Illustration took a course separate from the mainstream of fine art painting to remain colorful and pictorial. Maxfield Parrish and Norman Rockwell stand out as beloved illustrators of the period—Maxfield Parrish for his colorful fantasies and Norman Rockwell for depicting the humble and humorous moments in life.

More recently, several new art movements have emerged on the art scene: pop art, funk art, and photorealism. Pop art, initiated by Andy Warhol, introduced commercial art images like the famous Campbell's soup can into gallery painting. Photorealists revived an interest in realistic images made directly from photographs, and many chose to paint such symbols of modern culture as cars, street lights, signs, fast foods, suburban houses, and swimming pools. Funk art, developed on the west coast of the United States as a reaction to the drug culture of the 1960s, was a kind of surrealism with a sense of humor that revitalized interest in surrealism, fantasy, and conceptual art.

The women's movement of the 1970s contributed to a reevaluation of different forms of decorative art that had for many years been considered trivial and decadent. Painters began to experiment with decorative motifs from the American art of quiltmaking as well as from international sources such as Moslem mosaics. The term "pattern painting" was coined to describe the new decorative style of painting.

Meanwhile, abstract expressionism has continued to flourish in various new forms, and artists have recently renewed interest in impressionism and expressionism. The illustrative arts have flourished amid this activity. Revitalized by an influx of new ideas and encouraged by the wide range of styles and techniques encompassed in the art world, illustrative art is no longer alienated from the mainstream of activity as it was a few decades ago.

Current Trends

Today, the illustrative arts reflect a colorful variety of different styles. Among these, we can identify three recent trends in the field of illustration:

1. A trend toward conceptual art.
2. A new interest in realism.
3. An emphasis on personal style.

Many illustrators in all fields of illustration, from editorial to fashion, are interested in creating art that is conceptual. It is also a popular art trend in Europe. Rooted in the dada and surrealism of the 1900s, conceptual art is more than pleasing to look at: it also presents thought-provoking ideas to the viewer. The artist creates conceptual art by the manner in which images are arranged and designed, and it often resembles surrealistic or fantasy art in appearance, although all fantasy art is not necessarily conceptual.

The development of photography and photorealistic techniques has produced an increasing amount of detailed, realistic artwork. Photorealistic techniques are applied to surrealistic as well as to realistic imagery. Many different mediums, from acrylic paints sprayed with an airbrush to painted watercolors, are used to create detailed and illusionistic artwork.

The trend toward originality and intensely personal expression has resulted in a larger variety of illustrative styles and techniques than ever before. Artists feel free to experiment with realism, fantasy, impressionism, expressionism, and any other style, using a wide variety of artists' materials.

4 Eight variations on three pencils.

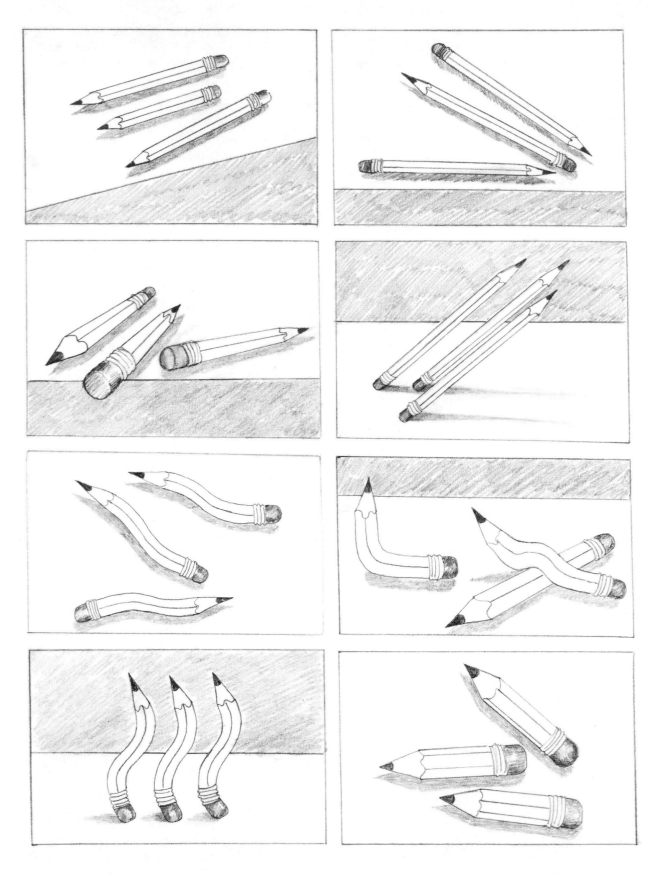

Chapter
one
Basic
Techniques

From start to finish an illustration will go through the following stages:

1. Thumbnail sketch. These are preliminary sketches that explore and determine the idea and composition of the illustration.
2. Rough drawing. This is a more finished line drawing in pencil or ink, completed in the correct proportions of the assignment. This drawing serves a professional purpose—to show your client what the final artwork will look like. In some instances, you may be asked to include color in your rough drawing. In that case, the rough drawing is called a "comprehensive."
3. Finished artwork. Later chapters describe different techniques that may be used for the final artwork.

This chapter describes the step-by-step techniques of making the thumbnail sketch and the rough drawing, preliminary drawings that serve to develop the original idea before the artist makes the finished artwork. They are the planning stages of an illustration and they are essential because even the simplest illustration must be well planned.

Getting to Know the Assignment

Illustrations are used in many different places: textbooks, book covers, magazines, newspapers, record album covers, and billboards, in thousands of variations and themes. However it is presented, an illustration is expected to communicate and to have impact. As an illustrator, you will need to get to know and understand each assignment so that you can do the best possible job. A professional illustration assignment will always provide the artist with the following information before sketching begins: (1) the subject of the illustration, including any written material it may accompany, such as a story, article, book, chapter, campaign slogan, and (2) the size and dimensions of the illustration.

It is a good idea for a student to work with restrictions similar to those in a typical illustration assignment: a specific subject matter and a set of dimensions. Some suggested subjects and sizes are given in the exercises at the end of this chapter. A classroom situation can provide the additional learning experience of seeing the different ways students illustrate the same subject.

Subject matter can range from simple to complex. To familiarize yourself with it, read the material that you are given. If the subject is unfamiliar to you, you may want to study it in greater depth. Some specific subjects, such as portraits, products, and others, are discussed in *Chapter Five*.

For now, let us make the distinction between straightforward and interpretive subjects. The straightforward subject is specific, "a couch" or "a hand pulling a zipper" or "a dog." No interpretation of the subject itself is required by the artist. On the other hand, the artist may be given a story to read and illustrate without instructions to depict a specific subject but with freedom to choose the idea, composition, and subject matter. In that case, the assignment is considered to have an interpretive subject. In interpretive illustration, more decisions are left up to the artist.

The size dimensions will be given with an illustration assignment. To sketch ideas for an illustration, you do not need the exact measurements, but a general idea is necessary. You can work in a larger size than the size of the finished artwork as long as you work in the correct proportions. For now, in order to make some thumbnail sketches (as in the following section), it is necessary to know only the shape of the composition. If the size dimensions are 6″ × 6″, 10″ × 10″, or 4″ × 4″, the composition is a square. If the size dimensions are 7″ (width) × 4″ (height), the composition is wider than it is tall, which is called a horizontal composition. If the size dimensions are 5″ (width) × 9″ (height), the composition is taller than it is wide and is called a vertical composition. The shape of the space—whether square, horizontal, or vertical—will affect the composition of an illustration. In a tall narrow space, you may choose to draw a standing figure. In a short wide space, you may decide to draw the figure lying down.

The Thumbnail Sketch

Materials Needed
- *Newsprint paper*
- *Soft pencil*

With a pencil, outline several areas on a large tablet of paper in the proportions of the shape desired for the finished illustration. If the composition is square, outline several squares; if it is vertical, outline several vertical rectangles, and so on. Draw a different idea in each box.

Be bold and adventurous as you make several sketches. Use a soft pencil and inexpensive paper, such as newsprint, so that you are uninhibited. Draw as many as you like. If your subject is a straightforward one, like a car, you can play with only the location of details, textures, and subtle composition changes.

If your subject is interpretive, you have many more decisions to make. First, you must decide what specific subject matter will be in the illustration and then determine how to arrange it in a composition. The best way to make these decisions is to sketch a few ideas and see how they look. Be prepared to throw many in the trash before you find one that looks reasonable. Don't actually throw any away until you have completed sketching; you may find a part of one or another that is worth saving.

If you are a beginner, keep your ideas as simple as possible. Some of the simplest subjects and compositions can be the most elegant.

What do you do if you cannot think of an idea for a sketch? Or if you conceived one idea but cannot come up with any other approach? Here are a few suggestions:

- Look at some of your favorite illustrations by other artists. Study the composition and treatment of the subject matter. Ask yourself what problems the artists faced, and how they solved them. Your illustration assignment will probably deal with different subject matter, but you may be able to use a similar treatment of the subject or a similar composition. Imitating is a natural part of the process of learning from others.
- Look through artistic photography books for ideas on composition. You can find such books, which may be expensive to

5

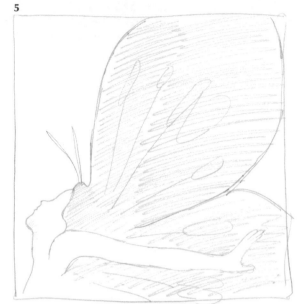

6

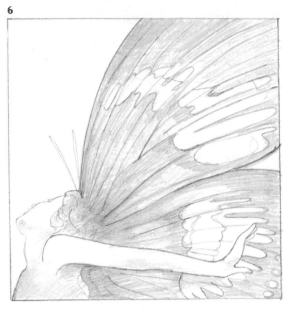

7

5 Thumbnail sketch: Butterfly Woman

6 Rough drawing: Butterfly Woman

7 Design for a cover illustration by Judy Olson. The idea of the design was kept intact yet altered to the artist's own style when a rough drawing was made from this design (*see* all stages of the Butterfly Woman).

8 A composition or design is balanced if the "weight" is evenly distributed. Here the large, dark dog on the righthand side of the composition outweighs the small mouse. The result is a design that looks unbalanced.

9 In this composition, the values and shapes are balanced. The large, white dog is balanced by a dark cat and a white mouse.

purchase, at the public library. Photographers spend a lot of time looking at the world through a frame in the camera, and they develop an excellent eye for composition. One of these compositions could inspire an idea for a thumbnail sketch.

• Try a visualization technique. Think about the subject you are going to illustrate, and picture in your mind everything you know about it. If you can visualize a scene, sketch it. Imagine the scene rearranging itself, and sketch that as well.

As you are thinking of ideas and arranging the composition, keep in mind what you have learned from drawing, design, or composition classes. The same principles that are taught in a fine-arts class apply to illustration. In other words, don't try to "think commercial" as you illustrate.

COMPOSITION TIPS

The elements necessary for good composition or design are balance and interest. Both are important in your illustration.

8

9

10 Symmetrical composition with perspective.

11 In this drawing the basic shape is symmetrical; the details are asymmetrical.

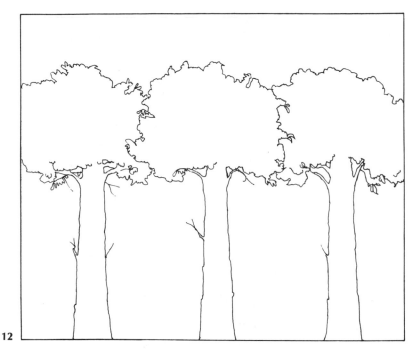

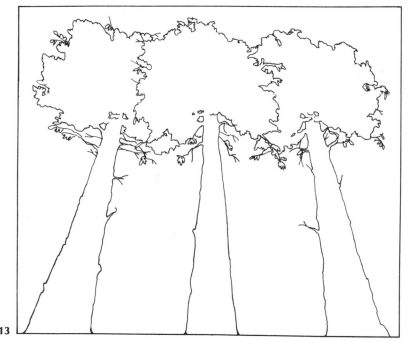

12 A horizontal and vertical composition.

13 The same composition as seen from a different perspective creates diagonal lines in the composition. Drawing with perspective will always create diagonal lines and a greater sense of action as the eyes move in and out of the perspective line.

A composition or design is balanced if the "weight" is evenly distributed. Large objects and dark objects "weigh" the most; small objects and light-colored objects "weigh" the least. Imagine that the page is a scale. If all the objects on the left side of the page are large and/or dark and all the objects on the right side of the page are small and/or light, the scale would tip, and the large objects would fall off the page.

How do we balance the scale? One obvious way is to plan a symmetrical composition in which the two halves mirror each other if you draw a line down the center. For example, a face placed in the center of a page is a symmetrical composition. A house in the center of the drawing with a small tree on one side and a small dog on the other side is also a symmetrical composition. In this case, the small dog and the small tree are the same height, and they balance the scale and composition.

There are many other ways to make a balanced composition. For example, a small, dark-colored object on one side of a drawing can be balanced with a large, light-colored object on the other side, if they are the same "weight." It is also possible to balance weight on a diagonal line running from one corner of the drawing to the other, if the two triangles of the drawing mirror each other. For example, a house on the lower left-hand side of the drawing may be balanced by a large moon on the upper right-hand side of the drawing.

Simply put, a composition is balanced when the subjects in a drawing do not look as if they are going to fall off one side of the page or the other. The page will have a sense of stability that makes it easy to look at. An unbalanced composition will give the viewer a feeling of uneasiness.

The composition and design should also be interesting. You can give your composition interest by using a variety of textures, by drawing contrasting shapes, by using interesting colors, or by varying the lines and forms in the artwork. Techniques for implementing these suggestions are discussed throughout the book.

14

Another element that adds interest to a composition is motion. Subjects that form horizontal or vertical lines in a composition are said to be "quiet" and have little motion. Imagine a drawing of a flat desert landscape, with vertical telephone poles beside a long, horizontal highway. The lines these subjects make are horizontal and vertical, and they create a stable, quiet composition.

15

Subjects that form diagonal or curved lines create the greatest feeling of motion. A hill drawn on a diagonal, a rocket flying on a diagonal, and a kite string on a diagonal are all active subjects which are less restful to the eye than horizontal and vertical lines. Curved lines, like those created by a dragon's tail curling behind the beast, a curving road, or a flowing dress, are both active *and* soothing to the eye.

16

The purpose of the thumbnail sketch is to try out many ideas. Even if the subject is straightforward, you will want to sketch it with subtle variations. Choose the sketch you like the best, and then you are ready to make a rough drawing.

14 A horizontal and vertical composition.

15 The same composition with a sense of perspective. The perspective creates diagonal lines in the illustration and makes it more active.

16 A diagonal composition. This arrangement is the most active of the three compositions depicting bicycles.

17 Vertical composition.

18 Horizontal composition.

17

18

The Rough Drawing

Materials Needed
- *Drawing paper*
- *Ruler*
- *Pencil*
- *Ink pen (optional)*
- *Colored pencils (optional)*
- *Watercolors (optional)*
- *Source material*

The next step is to improve and refine the ideas in the thumbnail sketch in a more developed drawing called the "rough." Illustration assignments almost always require you to submit a rough for approval because the client wants to get an idea of what you have planned before you proceed to the final artwork. This is the stage at which changes are made, if necessary. Sometimes two or more rough drawings are requested so that the client may choose among them. In that case, the illustrator is paid for the extra roughs as well as for the final artwork. The rough drawing will have to sell your idea to a client, so it should be your best effort.

A rough is made in the same shape and proportions designated for the final product. It is drawn in pencil or ink, using

19 20 21 22 Several rough drawings were made for a shoe campaign for "Foot Gear." Two were chosen to be made into finished art.

20

22

21

a simple technique. The drawing should look neat and well-rendered, although it will not include much time-consuming detail. Textures will be only suggested. The rough is the bare bones of a drawing, but it should look handsome nonetheless.

SIZE

It is best to make your rough drawing, and later the finished artwork, the same size specified for the reproduction, or slightly larger, but no more than twice that size. There is an advantage to working larger than the reproduction size: when the artwork is reduced, it may look crisper and sharper in detail. However, this is true only up to a point; working larger than twice the size may have the opposite effect, as the artwork begins to lose some of its detail if it is reduced a great deal.

Reducing the artwork is a simple, inexpensive, photographic process. However, it is important that the working size be in *exact* proportion to the reproduction size. For example, if the given size of the illustration is 4″ × 6″, you can make the artwork 5″ × 7½″, 6″ × 9″, or 8″ × 12″, because all of these sizes are in proportion to 4″ × 6″. If 4″ × 6″ is converted to the fraction 4/6, and reduced to ⅔, it can be used to ascertain all of the sizes that are in proportion to 4″ × 6″ by multiplication: 3/3 × 2/3 = 6/9, or the size dimensions 6″ × 9″; 4/4 × 2/3 = 8/12, or the size dimensions 8″ × 12″; 1.5/1.5 × 2/3 = 5/7.5, or the size dimensions 5″ × 7½″; and so on.

23 Make your artwork in proportion to the dimensions of the reproduction size. Draw a square or rectangle the size of the given assignment and then draw a diagonal line through the corners of it. Make a larger rectangle by drawing parallel lines to the diagonal. All rectangles which are made along the diagonal will be in proportion to the original size. For example, if this rectangle represents 4″ × 6″, then another rectangle 6″ × 8″ will be in correct proportion to it.

Another way to find a size in proportion to the original is to make a simple diagram. Using a ruler, draw a square or rectangle the size of the given dimensions. Extend two sides of the rectangle to the approximate size that you would like to do the artwork. Draw a diagonal line through the opposite corners and extend it beyond the rectangle. Now draw lines outside the original rectangle that are parallel to the rectangle and intersect the diagonal line. You will make a larger rectangle that is in exact proportions to the original one.

By intersecting the diagonal line within the original rectangle, you will make a smaller rectangle, and by intersecting farther out on the diagonal, you will make a larger one. As long as the diagonal line is intersected, you can be certain that the size is exactly in proportion to the original.

Instead of using the methods above to compute the correct proportions of the artwork to the reproduction size, you may

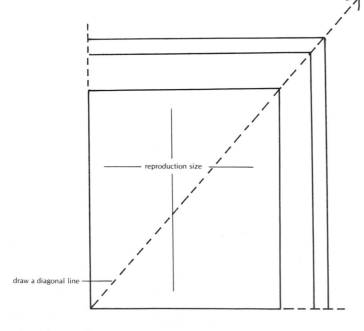
reproduction size

draw a diagonal line

choose to use a proportional scale wheel. This tool, which looks like a plastic wheel, can be purchased at an art or drafting supply store. It is especially useful for making difficult computations which include accuracy to the fraction of an inch.

The reproduction size of the artwork is numbered on the outer edge of the wheel. Inside these figures is a rotating wheel printed with the original size numbers. With two of these figures lined up together, a window displays the corresponding percentage of the two as well as the number of times the artwork must be reduced to become the reproduction size. Let's say you are given the reproduction size of 6″ × 7½″ and you would like to work larger than this, within an optimal range of 60–90% reduction of the original. When 75% is in the window display, the outer wheels will align 6″ and 7½″ with 8″ and 10″.

Choose a working size that suits your particular bent—within reasonable limits.

If you feel free only when you work very large, by all means do so. Several professional illustrators paint on canvas that requires reduction of 400 percent or more! However, it is not a good idea to work smaller than the reproduction size. Although artwork can be photographically blown up to any size, it will become granular, and the quality will suffer.

While planning the size of your illustration in the rough drawing, you must sometimes allow for ''bleed'' by making the artwork a little larger because, for one reason or another, the edges of an illustration will be cut off. They may be masked by a

24 The outer lines in this figure indicate the borders of the actual illustration and the inner lines indicate how the drawing will be trimmed. Allow at least ¼″ extra on all four sides of a drawing, since this area will be trimmed off in the printing process.

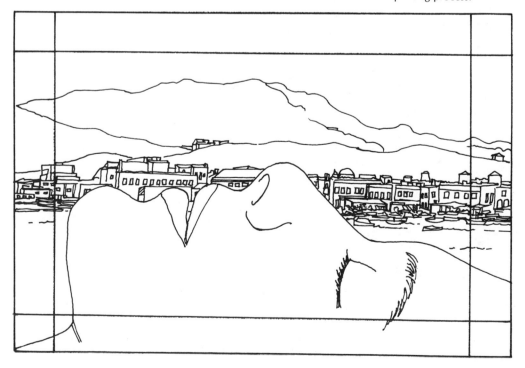

window, framed in a border, or run off the edge of a page and trimmed. In any case, you will lose the edges of your artwork, so you must plan for it. Add ½" to any edge that will bleed, and do not draw or paint an important element of the illustration near these edges. If, for example, the dimensions of an illustration which is to bleed on all four sides are 4" × 6", the minimum size for a rough drawing, and later the final artwork, would be 4½" × 6½".

The only kind of illustration that does not require allowance for bleed is a silhouette that floats on the page. If the figure is self-contained and surrounded by white space, none of the drawing will be lost when the page is trimmed. The cover illustration of this book is an example of a silhouette.

MATERIALS & TECHNIQUE

The materials and technique used for the rough drawing depend upon the medium you will be using for the final artwork. If the final artwork is to be a simple line drawing in pen-and-ink, pencil line work should be used for the rough. Use a soft pencil on drawing paper so that the line is dark enough to be seen easily but light enough so that you can still make changes and correct mistakes.

If the final illustration is to be done in watercolors, colored pencils, or acrylics, the rough drawing should suggest tone and shading. Using a soft pencil, sketch in the dark and middle values and indicate any texture in the illustration. Use the side of your pencil to make a smooth tone.

Colored pencils or watercolors are good techniques to use if you are asked to include color in the rough drawing. Both can be applied quickly. Use the same color scheme and the approximate intensity of colors planned for the final artwork. The difference is that you do not have to be as careful with your technique or as detailed. See the sections in *Chapter three* on colored pencils and watercolors for more information on these techniques.

If the final artwork is elaborate enough to demand two to four weeks of the artist's time, a more sophisticated rough drawing known as a "comprehensive" may be requested. Artists often use a combination of colored pencils and acrylic paint to supply the color and detail expected in a comprehensive, because the technique looks good but can be executed fairly quickly. General areas of color are covered with acrylics, and colored pencils are used to add values, detail, and depth on top of the paint. For more on this technique, see the section on colored pencils in *Chapter three*.

IMPROVING THE DRAWING

One way to improve your idea is to add more detail and definition to the drawing. Where does an artist look for more information? There are three major sources: (1) drawing from memory, (2) drawing from life, and (3) drawing from photographs. To decide which method is best for you, let's examine each one. (You may also decide to use a combination of the three.)

Drawing from Memory.   While drawing from memory, you depend on the storehouse of information in your mind, which is usually not stocked with much visual detail. As you look around every day, you see so much that your mind cannot possibly record every detail, so it often perceives things as symbols and generalities. For example, if you glance at a crowd of people, you will first recognize the shape and movement that make you think ''a crowd of people.'' It would take more than a quick glance to notice faces, color of hair, color of clothing, and so on, and indeed many activities in daily life do not require us to notice *exactly* what things look like.

You notice a traffic light when it turns red or green because the color affects whether you stop your car or walk across the street. However, for all those countless times you have looked at a traffic light, do you remember exactly what the light itself looks like? Do you remember the exact shape, how it is mounted, or what color is on top?

Some things, like a new car or a pretty face, invariably catch our eye during daily activities. In general, people and faces attract our attention more than most subjects, but a great part of what we notice about them is not recorded in detail.

The pitfall of drawing from memory is the danger of producing an illustration that is so simplified and generalized that it is uninteresting. There is also the problem of having so little information about a particular subject in your memory that the drawing simply looks wrong. If you want to draw from memory, you must train yourself to:

1. Become more observant in your daily life by noticing as much detail as possible and studying the lines, shapes, and textures of what you see.
2. Use your imagination when drawing from memory and be as inventive as possible.

Cartooning is a fast-paced style of illustration and often requires an artist to draw from memory. Objects and people are simplified by using shapes and symbols. There is good cartooning and bad cartooning. Bad cartooning is simple and dull and looks like something you've seen before, like that ''happy smile face.'' Good cartooning, however, is an exciting art form, which shows character and originality through the artist's inventive use of simple shapes and symbols.

It is natural to draw from memory for thumbnail sketches. They require free associating and a fast technique. But for the rough drawing, you may choose to draw from life or from a photograph.

Drawing from Life or from a Photograph.   Drawing from life means drawing a subject while you look at it. The subject may be an object or a model in your studio or a scene in the park. The prerequisite for drawing from life is that your subject be accessible. Some subjects—like a satellite passing Jupiter—are simply not available for observation.

The best subjects are small ones like household items and clothing, which can be propped up in front of you. If you are willing to sketch outside of your studio, you will find interesting subjects at the zoo or in the park or around your neighborhood. If you need a figure in your illustration, you may ask a friend or relative to hold a short pose. For a long pose, you can hire a professional model, but that is costly. It may be more practical to take a snapshot of a friend to save time and money.

Drawing from life is a direct, personal way to draw. The characteristics of the subject are there for you to observe firsthand. For example, if you want to draw an old baseball glove, what better way is there than to have one in front of you? You can observe the details that give the glove character—the finger lacing, the texture of the leather, and the cracks and crevices from wear. These details and the way you draw the subject make the illustration a unique interpretation. Although drawing from life may be as detailed as drawing from a photograph, it is usually less exacting. Two artists' drawings of the same live subject will differ more than their illustrations drawn from the same photograph. Greater freedom of interpretation contains the possibility of distorting the subject in an interesting, individual way.

Whether you choose to draw from life or not will depend on how you want to present the subject matter. If the illustration calls for a personal or interpretive treatment, drawing from life would be a good technique. If the illustration must be very accurate, an exact duplication of the client's product, for example, it may be helpful to use a photograph.

Some subjects cannot be drawn from life. Small children and animals won't sit still, and celebrities like the President cannot spare an afternoon. For subjects like these and others not found in your own neighborhood, you will need a photograph.

Drawing from life is more difficult than drawing from a photograph because the subject is three-dimensional and the drawing is two-dimensional. Beginners should start with simple photographs and take classes in still life and figure drawing if they wish to pursue it. (Photography is discussed in detail in the next section.)

Photography as a Tool

Drawing from a photograph is convenient because the camera has done some of the work for you by transforming the subject into a two-dimensional image. The perspective and proportions of objects captured by the camera's eye are true to life in a photographic sense, and if you have a time limit, it is helpful to have them worked out for you. However, photography should not be viewed as an easy way out, but rather as a place to begin. Drawing or tracing from a photograph can be a shortcut that provides time for you to develop and improve the drawing further.

Photographs are available from many sources. You can take your own photographs, or you can find them in picture books or magazines at a public library. The library is the best place to look up unusual subjects, because in addition to the encyclopedias, picture books, and magazines dating back 10 to 20 years, most libraries have picture files. Among all these sources, you are bound to find pictures of nearly any subject imaginable.

25 Photographs were supplied by the client for the "Foot Gear" campaign. Even though much of the illustration is fanciful, the representation of the shoes themselves is accurate.

In the rare instance when the picture cannot be checked out, you can take your sketch pad to the library and work there.

You may want to start a picture-book and old magazine collection. It is convenient to own old magazines because you can cut out pictures to manipulate on the page or to use in a collage technique (described in *Chapter five*. Many people who throw old magazines in the trash would be willing to save them for you instead. Thrift shops sell them for next to nothing. Once you have accumulated a collection, it is a good idea to organize the magazines by subject categories for easy reference. Use general categories, such as "nature" for magazines like *National Geographic, The Sierran,* or *Travel,* and "people" for magazines such as *Time, Newsweek,* or *People.* Other categories might be "sports," "humor," "food," "crafts," and so on.

It can be useful to know how to be your own photographer, whether you use a simple Instamatic camera or more sophisticated equipment. A Polaroid camera is handy for snapshots of a subject that you need to draw immediately, and it is convenient because you don't have to develop an entire roll of film for one or two pictures. On the other hand, the image from the Polaroid picture will tend to be small and difficult to trace.

With an Instamatic or 35mm camera, you have the choice of taking prints or color slides. Prints are a good choice if you want to study and draw the subject freehand. However, if you want to trace the subject, you will probably need to enlarge the print to the size of the illustration. Many graphic houses have a Luci, a machine used to enlarge or reduce images. It works like an opaque projector, except that it enlarges the image in a range practical for the illustrator, which varies according to the individual machine. A Luci is handy to have, but it may be more expensive than most free-lance artists can afford.

Color slides are another answer if you want to trace from your own photographs. They are less expensive to develop than prints and can be projected to any size with a slide projector.

If your illustration calls for figures in various positions, consider setting up a scene with friends or paid models holding the pose for the illustration. If you take a print or slide of the scene, the models will have to hold the pose only a moment. This scene-staging method can produce a highly original illustration. Maxfield Parrish worked this way. In fact, he used himself as a model in some illustrations.

PROJECTING & TRACING TECHNIQUES

Now that you know how to find photographs, let us consider the technique of using them, in particular, projecting or tracing from a photograph. The tracing techniques described here can also be applied to tracing freehand drawings or transferring the design of the rough drawing onto drawing paper or illustration board for the final artwork.

Tracing from a Slide Projector. A slide projector enlarges an image from a slide as it projects it onto a screen. The focal length, or the distance from the projector to the screen, will determine the size of the projected image. The greater the focal length, the larger the image. The projector must be very close to the screen to create a small image.

A wall or board will do as well as a screen when you project for tracing. Tape your drawing paper onto this surface at a comfortable height for drawing. The paper should have a frame (the same dimensions as the illustration) lightly sketched on it in pencil. Use this frame to guide the projected image to the right location. You can fill the entire frame with the projected image, or you can direct the image to a particular location in the frame if you have other plans for the rest of the composition.

Project the slide onto the drawing paper, and adjust the focus and the distance of the projector from the wall until the subject is the right size for the illustration. With the lights dimmed so that the image appears crisp, sketch the outlines of the image *very lightly* with a pencil. In the dark, it is easy to press harder than you mean to, but a very light guideline is most desirable. The amount of detail you include is up to you. You may choose to outline only the basic proportions of the image or to spend an hour or more drawing the small details.

When the lights are on, your drawing should look like a maze of lightly penciled guidelines. These will be covered up as you finish the illustration with pencil, pen and ink, or paints.

Tracing with a Light Table. It is easier to trace the image in a photograph or drawing on a sunny window pane than on an opaque table. The sun shining through the glass makes the paper transparent and brightens the image. This principle is applied in the design of a light table, which can be conveniently used on your desk. A light table is basically a light bulb mounted under a glass plate supported in a frame. Turning on the light has the same effect as the sun in the window. A photo or drawing can be placed on the light table, with drawing paper on top, and traced.

Light tables come in different sizes, and prices begin around $100. However, you can make a workable light table for much less, even if you are not a carpenter or a mechanical engineer.

First, buy a piece of glass approximately 18″ × 24″ in size. Frosted glass or plexiglass, which diffuses light evenly and prevents glare, are excellent, but clear glass, which is cheap and easy to find, is fine. Wrap masking tape lengthwise around all four sharp edges of the glass, and continue adding layers until the glass is well-protected and safe to handle. This plate will be the drawing surface of the light table.

Make two even stacks of books or bricks on your desk to support the ends of the glass, leaving an area directly below it for a light. The glass plate should be about 5 inches from the desk. Position a small lamp or a flexible desk light to shine at an upward angle, and you are ready to trace on the light table.

Tracing with Graphite Paper. Graphite paper is a thin paper that works like carbon paper. The difference is that it releases graphite, which is erasable, instead of ink when it is pressed. It may be used to transfer a rough to drawing paper or illustration board for the final artwork or to trace a photograph. Graphite paper goes under the image to be traced, graphite side down on the drawing paper, and the tracing is done on top of the image.

Whenever you use this paper, you must test to find the degree of pressure needed to produce a barely visible guideline. The pressure will vary, depending on the weight of the paper you are drawing through. It is important not to press too hard, because the unsightly dark line that results is heavy and difficult to erase. Furthermore, a wet medium, such as watercolors, will not accept heavy graphite lines. If you do press too hard, erase as much as possible before you continue tracing.

REDUCING WITH A COPY MACHINE

Suppose you have a photograph suitable for your illustration, but it is too large. Or suppose you make a sketch of a figure from life, but it is too big to fit inside the dimensions of the illustration. In these situations, you can reduce the photograph or drawing in a copy machine in a fraction of the time it would take to redraw it freehand. Many copy machines found in business supply stores, libraries, and schools will make reductions of approximately 30 and 60 percent. If these settings do not reduce your photo or drawing enough, you can put the reduced copy into the machine to reduce it once again.

For the best reproduction on a copier, your drawing should have dark lines. It may be necessary to trace the photo with bold guidelines and to reduce the tracing instead of the photo. If your original drawing has strong lines, the reduced copies will be clear enough to trace or transfer to a drawing.

IS PHOTOGRAPHY "CHEATING"?

Some people think that "real" artists walk through life in a dream state, never studying the world around them, then sit down at an easel and paint nature as true and wonderful as it is. The truth is that through the ages the best artists have had to study their subjects carefully, traveling through the countrysides they painted, learning anatomy, and even dissecting cadavers to discover and understand more about their subjects. The invention of the camera gave artists one more means of exploring nature.

Art has been profoundly affected by the development of photography through the decades. As photography began to replace painting as the primary method of recording people and events, the art world turned to explore new areas of abstraction. Turn-of-the-century expressionists studied snapshots to explore new ideas about composition, as art and artists struggled for a new identity. It has been suggested that the total rejection of realistic art by twentieth-century abstract expressionists was an extreme reaction to the growing popularity of photography and the realism it recorded so well.

Recent years have seen a renewed interest in realism, and the term "photorealism" has been coined for painting very precisely and directly from a photographic source. The best photorealistic artwork is an enormous improvement over the original photo.

Now photography has become an art in its

own right, and the fine artists of both schools have joined forces over the years to share what each has to offer. The artist–illustrator should not hesitate to make use of photography in any way that may be helpful.

There is nothing wrong with copying a photograph to the last detail if the photo is your own. If you take the picture, it is yours to draw from, copy, or trace. However, if you use a photograph from a magazine or book, you will probably need permission from the photographer or owner of the photograph to trace or copy it. In any event, the photo should not be drawn exactly as it is—not only for reasons of legality and fairness, but to encourage your own originality. Some

change must be made in the composition, style, or imagery so that your illustration looks substantially different from any photograph that is not your own.

There are many ways to draw from a photograph that permit you to inject your own personality into the image without copying it entirely. You can copy a part of the photo and make up the rest, or you can use more than one photo in a collage technique (described in *Chapter five*). Another possibility is to use a style that is painterly or textured to alter the strict realism of the subject. Stippling with an ink pen or colored pens (*Chapter three*) is a technique that naturally abstracts an image so that it will look very different from the photo.

The Role of the Designer

A designer determines what an entire page or book will look like. This includes choosing the type and arranging the type and artwork on a page. It may be up to the designer to choose the illustrations or photographs for the page. For this reason, it is often a designer who hires the illustrator.

In some instances, the designer will want a subject so specific that he or she will provide a rough drawing of the planned illustration. The work of thinking up an idea and composition is thus already done for the artist, who is hired only to apply skill and technique, which the designer may lack, to the finished illustration.

Often the skills of designer and illustrator overlap. For our purposes throughout this book, we assume that the illustrator has the responsibility of designing the illustration as well as finishing it with a skillful technique.

In this chapter we have gone through the steps of making a thumbnail sketch and a rough drawing. The rough drawing for an illustration can be compared to the blueprints for a house. It is the plan. The decisions you make and how you plan affect the success of the illustration. The next chapters will describe the many different techniques that you can employ to finish the illustration.

26 Finished artwork: Butterfly Woman
Artist: Marta Thoma
Client: St. Martin's Press
Media: Watercolors and acrylics

1. Draw a tree, a house, or a face in all three of the following ways:
   - From memory.
   - From life.
   - From a photograph.

2. Choose a straightforward subject such as a hat, a chair, or a book in the dimensions 6″ × 6″, and do the following:
   - Make three thumbnail sketches.
   - Make a rough drawing.

3. Choose an interpretive subject such as a poem or a short story with the dimensions of the illustration given as 8″ (width) × 10″ (depth), and do the following:
   - Make six thumbnail sketches.
   - Make a rough drawing.

4. Choose an interpretive subject such as a book or short story title, with the dimensions of the illustration given as 9″ (width) × 7″ (depth), and do the following:
   - Make six thumbnail sketches.
   - Draw a comprehensive with color for the illustration.

5. If the dimensions of an illustration are given as 8½″ (width) × 11″ (depth), what are six other possible sizes you can make the artwork? Remembering that you must allow for bleed in the artwork, what is the minimum size your artwork can be?

27 Artist: Marta Thoma
Portrait of Barbara Streisand.

Chapter
two
The Simple
Line Drawing &
Variations

The most basic illustrating technique is pen-and-ink, and the simplest pen-and-ink drawing is a line illustration. Line art is popular because it is fast and simple to draw, inexpensive to reproduce, and reduces well. Pen-and-ink drawings are used in newspaper cartoons and illustrations because the bold lines hold up even on newsprint, a poor quality paper. Other more delicate mediums like watercolors, which have intermediate gray tones, will not reproduce as well on poor quality paper. You may have noticed that the best-looking graphics in newspapers, including photographs, have a bold quality.

It is the absence of middle gray tones that make ink line drawings inexpensive to reproduce. Because they are black on white, pen-and-ink drawings do not entail the expense of film costs involved in reproducing by halftone photography. Gray tones require a halftone shot of the artwork, which is a photograph taken through a screen to produce the dotted texture necessary to hold the ink as it prints on the press. You have probably

29

Great Performances celebrates

Ormandy at 80

It's birthday time for Eugene Ormandy—and there's a gift for everyone as the maestro conducts the Philadelphia Orchestra in Rachmaninoff's Second Symphony and talks about his 44 years behind the baton.

Tonight 9:00/Ch. Thirteen PBS
Simulcast on WNCN/104.3 FM Stereo
Tomorrow at 8:00 PM on WNYC/Ch. 31 PBS

28

28 Artist: Burt Silverman
Client: Exxon
Title: *Ormandy at 80*
Art Director: Susan Lyster
Media: Pen-and-ink
This simple but elegant portrait of Eugene Ormandy was made with a combination of crosshatching and textured line work. The black background silhouettes the gesture of the conductor and dramatically outlines his snow-white hair.

29 Artist: Marta Thoma
Title: *Five O'Clock*
Media: Pen-and-ink

noticed the dotted texture of newspaper photographs shot through a coarse screen. Artwork and photographs reproduced on quality paper are usually shot through a much finer screen so that you cannot see the dotted pattern.

Since it is a bold medium, pen-and-ink line drawing also reduces well. The lines get stronger as they are reduced, and there is little worry of losing detail. This gives you the freedom to work much larger than the reproduction size.

Materials

There are two methods of doing a line drawing. For one you will use drawing paper, for the other, illustration board. When choosing a drawing paper, look for lightweight paper with the smooth, hard surface known as "hot-pressed". A "cold-press" paper has a textured quality that may cause the ink to bleed and make a fuzzy line. Look for the same hot-pressed quality in an illustration board, and choose one that has a smooth, hard finish.

To make a line illustration, we will start with a rough drawing you made in the last chapter. Method #1 below requires a store-bought or homemade light table for transferring the rough drawing design. For Method #2 below, you will need graphite paper to make the transfer to illustration board. You can make a substitute for graphite paper by rubbing one side of a thin piece of paper with pencil.

Use a fine-line, felt-tip pen for drawing. The size of most such pens corresponds approximately to a cartridge size 2 pen or a speedball pen, point tip size B6.

Method #1

Materials Needed
- *Rough drawing*
- *Drawing paper*
- *Light table*
- *Tape*
- *Fine-line, felt-tip pen*

Tape the rough drawing to the light table so that it will not slip, and tape over it a piece of drawing paper large enough to provide at least a couple of inches of border space around the illustration. When you finish, you can use the border space for handling and mounting the art. The light table should make the drawing paper transparent enough to trace the design. Since the design is bright and clear, you will be able to draw the ink lines with flowing, confident strokes.

Method #2

Materials Needed
- *Rough drawing*
- *Illustration board*
- *Graphite paper*
- *Tape*
- *Fine-line, felt-tip pen*

Tape the graphite paper, coated side down, on the illustration board, and tape the rough drawing on top of it. To test the amount of pressure you need to apply, slip a piece of scrap paper under the two layers and practice making a *very light* guideline with a sharp pencil. When you are confident that you know the correct pressure, retrace the design of the rough, pressing its image onto the illustration board. The graphite guidelines on the board must be redrawn with the felt-tip pen after you finish. The pen strokes should be smooth and flowing.

What if you make a mistake in ink? First allow it to dry, then cover the line that you would like to correct with the white paint that is used for correcting typewriting errors, painting it on with the small brush provided. The white paint may not match the white paper perfectly, but the two whites will fade together when the artwork is reproduced, and the mistake will vanish.

Variations on the Simple Line Drawing

One way to elaborate on the simple pen-and-ink line drawing is to add textures and tones to enhance the illustration. Let's look at some of the techniques that are used and the materials that are necessary.

A fine-line, felt-tip pen has its uses, but it also has limitations: (1) it will make only one size line, and the pen is not available in many sizes, (2) the ink supply is not long lasting, and (3) the quality of the ink is inferior to artist's ink, which causes the artwork to fade quickly and become a light blue color in a year or two. This may not be of any consequence, since most illustrations are needed for one-time reproduction only. If, however, you want the artwork to last, whether it is for yourself or for a second reproduction in the future, it is best to use a dip pen or cartridge pen with ink of lasting quality.

The Dip Pen.   The dip pen and the cartridge pen are popular tools which make excellent pen-and-ink artwork. The dip pen is less expensive. It has a wooden handle that fits onto a variety of different

30

31

30 Crosshatching with textural lines.

31 Textural lines.

32 Countoured crosshatching.

33 Stippling.

34 Textural lines.

35 Textural lines.

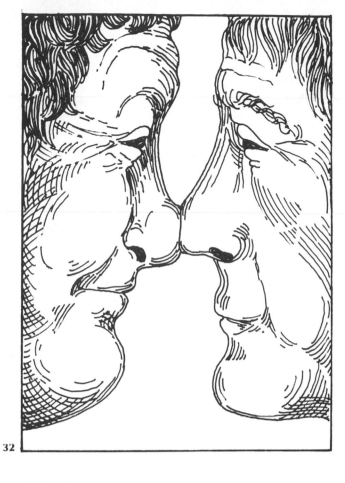

32

33

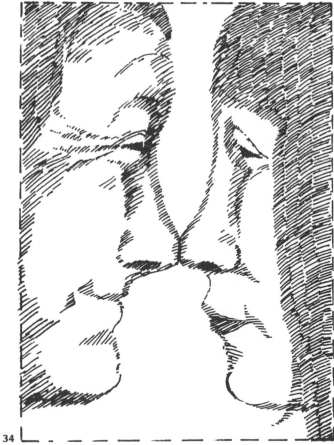

34

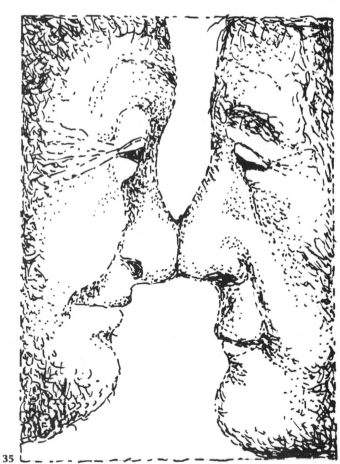

35

pen tips, which are sold separately. The pen tips range from very-fine quill tips to broader types. The metal on the tip is split so that with increased pressure of your hand, ink flows more rapidly from the pen. Hence you can make a variable line from thin to thick by varying the pressure of your hand. This is in contrast to the cartridge-style pen, which makes a gothic line of even width.

Ink for the dip pen is also sold separately. "Very Black" water-soluble ink is convenient because spills can be cleaned up easily. Waterproof ink has a richer appearance, and it is a must if you plan to use any ink or watercolor washes on top of the drawing: the lines will resist a water medium washed over them and will remain intact. Water-soluble ink, on the other hand, will bleed if it comes in contact with water, even after the ink has dried.

Care must be exercised in handling a dip pen, to avoid dripping the ink. Allow the excess to run off against the side of the jar each time the pen is dipped. It is helpful to test the first strokes on scrap paper to be sure that the pen has the right amount of ink for an even flow.

The Cartridge Pen.   A cartridge pen contains a reservoir of ink inside it, as a ballpoint pen does. Although it is more mechanical than the classic dip pen, it is very convenient because it releases a steady flow of ink. It does require a certain amount of care, but refilling and cleaning need not be done more often than every two weeks with frequent use.

If you use your pens every day, the frequent use will keep the pens flowing. If you don't, you will have to take steps to keep the ink from drying and clogging the tips. There are several different brands of cartridge pens, and each recommends a different method of keeping the pen lubricated when not in use. In one method, the pens are kept tip down inside a plastic capsule. A few drops of a humectant (a substance that retains moisture) are placed at the bottom of each of the slots that hold the pens. If the capsule lid is closed tightly over the pen set, the humectant will keep the pens moist and the ink flowing. Now and then the humectant will have to be refilled. The method I favor calls for a drop of water inside the specially designed cap of each pen. An indicator on the outside of the cap changes color when the water has evaporated to let you know when to add more water.

Pen tips come in sizes ranging from #00, the finest, to #6, which make a very broad line. The size you choose will be determined by the boldness and the percentage of reduction you want. For a delicate line drawing you might choose a #0 or #1 tip. However, the same effect can be produced by using a #3 tip and reducing the artwork by 100 percent. This technique produces a delicate, detailed look in the final reproduction.

You can also create the effect you want by using more than one tip size to vary the breadth of the lines. A broader pen tip will make a heavier line for emphasis in particular areas of a drawing. Contrasting lines are sometimes used to create the illusion of distance in a drawing: heavy lines suggest that subjects are close to the picture frame, while fine lines (#00, 0) indicate subjects far off in the distance. The principle here is that an image like a distant mountain appears to fade into the horizon as the distance from the viewer increases.

36 Artist: Roland DesCombes
Art Director: Roland DesCombes
Media: Pen-and-ink
This illustration was made with a combination of crosshatching and textured lines. This technique gave Roland DesCombes the flexibility to draw the many different textures found in the room—sofa pillows, carpet, folds in the man's trousers, books. To model the images, DesCombes applied shades of gray ranging from delicate to densely crosshatched black shadows. The broad spectrum of values gives the illustration its depth and strength.

37

38

CROSSHATCHING

When nature is reduced to black and white, as it is in a black-and-white television set, images derive their substance from varying shades of gray, ranging from nearly black to white. These gray shades, called "values," help to distinguish one image from another and give the subjects depth. Simple line drawings describe only the shape and contour of a subject, but values can be added to create a sense of depth by crosshatching. This is a method of crisscrossing lines to make an abstract gray pattern that serves as a value. Different values are produced by varying the density of the crosshatching.

You will need to refer to your source materials—the subject itself or a photo—to decide where and how to draw the values. In every instance, there will be light sources which highlight some areas and produce shadows in others. Leave the paper white where the light falls, and draw the darkest values where shadows fall.

Mechanical Crosshatching. We use the term "mechanical crosshatching" to mean lines which are drawn perfectly straight, even for building up value on a curved subject. The lines are crossed horizontally, vertically, and diagonally at a variety of angles. The width and boldness of the lines and their density—their distance from each other—determine how dark a value is. If the crosshatched lines are sparse, they will create a light value. If they are close together, so that little of the white paper shows through, they create a dark value.

Mechanical crosshatching can be done with a straightedge, like a ruler, or freehand. Crosshatching with a

37 Artist: Marta Thoma
Client: *San Francisco Chronicle*

38 Artist: Marta Thoma
Client: *San Francisco Chronicle*

39 Artist: Robert Steiner
Title: Detail of *Expulsion*

40 Artist: Robert Steiner
Title: Detail of *Expulsion*

straightedge will look neat and precise, more "perfect" than freehand crosshatching. Since freehand lines are not as straight, the effect will be more casual and less mechanical.

The key to being adept at crosshatching is to be able to apply the value skillfully, with smooth transitions when necessary. To practice these skills, make a test strip of crosshatching on your drawing paper, within a rectangle 10″ (width) × 2″ (depth). Starting from white on the left side of the strip, make a sample of crosshatching that gradually becomes denser until it is nearly black on the right-hand side. Aim for a gradual transition from light to dark that includes at least three intermediate values. When you are finished, you should be able to make dotted lines through the test strip every 2″. These should demarcate at least five distinct values.

Contoured Crosshatching.   Contoured crosshatching is similar to the crosshatching described above, except

that the lines conform to the shape of the subject. If the subject is square and boxlike, the lines will be straight, as in mechanical crosshatching. If the subject is rounded or contoured, the lines will follow the contour or suggest the internal curve of the subject. Contoured crosshatching is a flowing, expressive technique.

Edward Sorel's caricture of Woody Allen (see page 104) is an excellent example of how expressive this technique can be. The lines follow the contour of the figure, his shoulder, curved thigh, and wispy hair. The lines give the subject volume and a lively feeling because they had been applied so vigorously. If you look closely, you will discover at least five different values created by the crosshatching in the illustration.

To practice contoured crosshatching, begin with a line drawing of a simple curved subject like an apple. Practice building up values to give the subject volume, while following the curved shape

41 Artist: Marta Thoma
Client: *San Francisco Chronicle*

42 Artist: Brad Holland
Title: *The Trench*
Media: Pen-and-ink

41

with your lines. Try drawing with a cautious, controlled curved line and then try a looser, more fluid style to see which method best suits your personality.

MAKING VALUES WITH TEXTURES

Crosshatching is not the only pattern used to add values to drawings. Almost any pattern that is repeated over and over with increasing and decreasing density can create values, whether it is composed of small dashes, dots, circles, swiggles, scribbles, or curlicues. Some illustrators employ a stylized version of crosshatching that produces a neat patchwork of the crisscrossed lines. One of these techniques is a repeated pattern of three short parallel lines.

An unusual texture may dramatically affect a subject. Consider the Edward Sorel caricature of Frank Sinatra that is made up of scribbles. Sinatra looks old and frowning in the illustration, and the scribbling technique adds to the disquieting mood.

Stippling is a method of bouncing the pen gently on the paper with a stiff arm motion to make small dots of ink. The ink dots are spread thinly in light areas and gathered densely in dark areas. An illustration done in this manner is airy and atmospheric. It looks as if you are viewing the subject through a snowfall. Although it is a time-consuming technique, the results are well worth the effort. A fine-line, felt-tip pen is best for stippling because other pen tips can get bent, splayed, or blunted.

43

Frank Sinatra

READY-MADE TEXTURES

To apply values to a line drawing quickly, you can buy ready-made textures, or "zip-a-tone." These are sheets of sticky-backed plastic, printed in many patterns, such as crosshatching, stripes, dots, dashes, and so on. Each pattern is available in varying densities, from light gray to almost black.

To apply zip-a-tone to a line drawing, first decide where the value should go. The zip-a-tone value must be applied within a defined hard-edged area. Cut a piece of the zip-a-tone slightly larger than the size of each area you want to cover. Peel off the protective wax paper from the back and lay the "zip" where you want it, then trim it carefully, using an X-acto knife with a #11 blade, to fit within the lines.

If more than one value is desired, choose two, three, or more different gray tones In a zip-a-tone pattern and note on your rough drawing where you plan to apply each one. This is how values are applied to comic strips.

Zip-a-tone is useful for quick graphic illustrations and cartoons but not well suited to more developed, artistic illustrations. Zip-a-tone's hard-edged effect has a more design-like quality, which makes value gradations and smooth transitions difficult.

43 Artist: Edward Sorel
Client: *Village Voice*
Title: *Frank Sinatra*
Media: Pen-and-ink

SCRATCHBOARD

In scratchboard, a white line is made on a black surface, instead of the reverse. The scratchboard itself is a white board coated with india ink, and the white line is made by using a pen to scratch through the ink surface to expose the board.

The Board. Scratchboard is also available as an unpainted white board coated with a fine layer of white chalk. If you purchase the unpainted scratchboard, you must paint waterproof black ink on the scratchboard.

A beginner may want to start with the prepared style of scratchboard. It is excellent for a composition that does not have large areas of white. There are two brands of ink-coated scratchboard for sale, one superior to the other. The better scratchboard is heavier, so there is no need to mount it, and it has a dull ink surface which scratches well, producing clean lines. The other scratchboard is lightweight and has a shiny ink surface which, for some reason, tends to chip and crack more easily.

If you prepare your own scratchboard, you will find that the unpainted ones are sometimes lighter and flimsier than the painted type. To keep the board from buckling while you work, mount the scratchboard, using rubber cement, on a piece of illustration board. Use short, quick strokes to paint the board with ink. Let it dry and paint on a second coat.

Preparing your own scratchboard gives you the option of painting the entire surface black or painting a design with the black ink and leaving some of the illustration white. If you choose to paint a

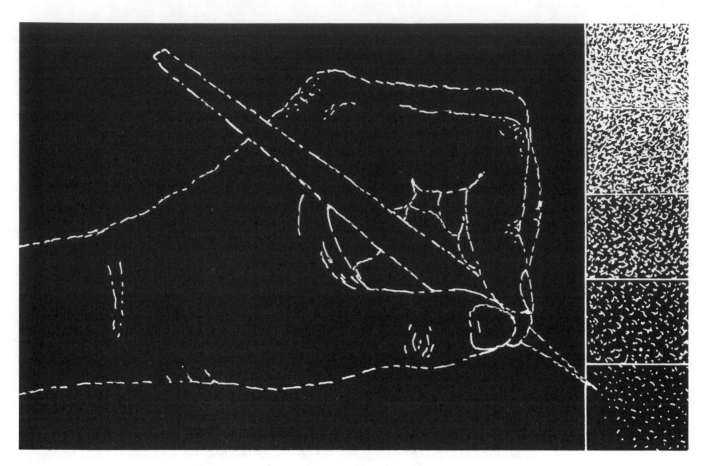

44 Using an etching tool on scratchboard to make tone in a textural and stippled technique.

design, work it out beforehand and sketch it in pencil on the white board. Let's say, for example, that your illustration is a portrait and you would like the figure to stand out dramatically in silhouette. You would first draw the subject lightly with pencil and then fill in the outline with ink, so it looks like a black shadow. You are now ready to draw on the inked surface with the techniques described next.

It is important to be able to draw a clean line through the ink on the scratchboard. There is nothing more discouraging than drawing a line that cracks and flakes off unevenly. To avoid this, buy the best brand of prepared scratchboard, and buy

artist's quality waterproof ink for the homemade board. These ink surfaces perform best in a warm, dry atmosphere. Cold and dampness have an adverse effect on the ink and cause it to chip more easily. Turn up the heat in your studio or work area on cold or rainy days when you are working with scratchboard.

Scratchboard Tools. Almost any sharp instrument that is comfortable to hold—an X-acto knife, for example—can be used as a scratching tool. Art stores sell inexpensive, fairly good tools that look like pen tips and slip into a pen holder for scratchboard work. The tips may be diamond-shaped, for a very fine line, or curved, to scoop off more ink and make a broader line.

An etching needle, which is sold where printmaking supplies are found, is excellent for cutting scratchboard. It is a sturdy tool made of metal, and it comes either with two pointed ends or with one sharp end mounted in a wooden handle. As it comes from the store, the point is shaped like the tip of a sharp knitting needle, which is better for drawing curves and flowing lines than the scratch pen tools. However, ends can be sharpened or dulled to your liking on an oil stone with a little oil. If you purchase an etching needle with two points, sharpen one end to cut fine lines and dull the other end to use for broader lines. Put corks on the sharp ends to protect the tool—and yourself—when you are not using it.

Scratchboard Techniques.   Hold the scratching tool in your hand like a pencil. Make a line by drawing toward yourself, not away. Practice making several lines in this way. Rotate the scratchboard on the table when necessary in order to maintain a comfortable hand position.

All of the line techniques previously discussed can be used on scratchboard—line drawing, crosshatching, texturing, and so on. The difference is that the line work is white on black instead of black on white. Typically, when you add crosshatching to a pen-and-ink drawing, you are adding values to the darkest areas, in the shade or shadows. To draw on scratchboard, you must think in reverse. Instead of adding shadows, you draw to create the light areas and highlights of the drawing. If the crosshatching is dense, the value will be light, and if the crosshatching is light, it will result in a dark value, just the opposite of pen-and-ink.

Practice straight and contoured crosshatching, stippling, and inventing textures with the cutting tools. Make a test strip of crosshatching that includes at least five distinct value changes. When you feel confident with crosshatching, try to draw a simple three-dimensional subject like an apple, using a picture or a real apple. Remember to leave the shadows and darkest areas black, and to include many different values in the drawing.

After you have practiced and you are ready to make an illustration, transfer a design of a rough drawing onto the scratchboard. Graphite paper works well for this. Lay the graphite paper face down on the scratchboard, place the rough drawing on top, and redraw the design. The graphite will show up as a shiny gray line on the black surface.

As you work into the drawing, refer to your source material for highlights and shadows. The lightest areas will be where the light is shining or reflecting. Drawing hair on people or animals is especially effective on scratchboard. It is natural to make a swiggly stroke for hair because that is how we think of it—as lots of little lines. The strokes are more effective in the scratchboard technique (light on dark) because highlights in hair are always light. By drawing denser lines where the light falls on the hair, you can create excellent highlights. If you were drawing in pen-and-ink (dark on light), the highlights would have to be left light, which is more difficult.

Mistakes can be touched up with ink to cover unwanted white lines. However, the repainted area is not as easy to draw into again because the original chalky surface has been scratched away. If necessary, you can even use white paint to touch up very small areas.

Consider combining scratchboard with pen-and-ink. Paint a design on unprepared scratchboard with ink, leaving some of the illustration board white and the design unfinished. Then scratch white lines into the black areas and draw black lines on the white areas. Aubrey Beardsley (1872–1898), the English artist noted for his work in black and white, made beautiful drawings using a combination of white designs on black next to black designs on white. It is worthwhile to study his drawings if you are interested in this striking kind of design.

Suggested Exercises

1. Make a simple line drawing using a rough drawing from *Chapter one* for the design.
2. Make a value test strip of mechanical crosshatching. Draw a rectangle 10″ long and 2″ tall on drawing paper. Working from left to right, increase the density of crosshatching so that the value progresses from light to dark. The change should take place gradually. When you are finished, you should be able to distinguish at least five different values in the test strip.
3. Begin with a line drawing of an apple. Then use contoured crosshatching to make the apple look three-dimensional. Refer to source materials, either a photo or a real apple.
4. Make a sample sheet of six different pen-and-ink techniques.
   - Using a pencil and ruler, draw a rectangle 8″ (width) × 12″ (depth). Then divide the rectangle into six even boxes, each 4″ square.
   - Cut a hole 2″ square in a piece of drawing paper. Place it on top of a photograph and move it around until it frames an interesting detail. When you are satisfied, tape the frame to hold it in place.
   - Draw the detail in the frame in each of the six boxes, using a different technique each time. Utilize the following techniques: (1) mechanical crosshatching using a ruler or straight edge, (2) mechanical crosshatching without a ruler, (3) contoured crosshatching, (4) stippling, (5) a texture (stripes, swiggles, dashes, and so on), and (6) a different texture.
   - Try to include at least five different values of each technique in each sample.
5. Make an illustration with one of the above techniques, using a rough drawing from *Chapter two* for the design. Refer to source material as you are drawing.
6. Make an illustration using zip-a-tone. Begin with a pen-and-ink line drawing. Purchase three different zip-a-tone values ranging from light gray to very dark gray. Decide where each should go by referring to source material if necessary. Apply the zip-a-tone, cutting away the excess with an X-acto knife.

7. Make an illustration on scratchboard, using a rough drawing from *Chapter one*. Transfer the drawing and use crosshatching or texturing to add values.

8. Using unprepared scratchboard, make an illustration that is a combination of scratchboard and pen-and-ink techniques. Do a rough drawing based on a short story or a topic that interests you. Paint part of the design in black and leave part of the design white. Scratch the details in the black parts to create white lines and add ink work to the white areas.

45 Artist: Marta Thoma
Client: St. Martin's Press
Media: Watercolors

Chapter
three
More
Illustration
Techniques

In this chapter we will explore a variety of different techniques to make an illustration. These techniques offer ways to add tone, color, and texture to your illustration, and each technique will give its own interesting quality to the artwork.

Although techniques for illustrating are as limitless as your imagination, I have included here those techniques which are used most often in the profession. As you will see, there are many to choose from.

Ink Wash

Tone can be added to a pen-and-ink line drawing quickly by diluting black ink with water to make the shades of gray washes desired and applying it as a wash. You cannot use this technique if the art has not been made with waterproof ink, because ink washes will smear and bleed if lines are made with water-soluble ink.

The other alternative is to make a separate overlay of ink washes on frosted acetate, which is registered to the line drawing. (See the section in this chapter on Color Separations for instructions on how to make an overlay.)

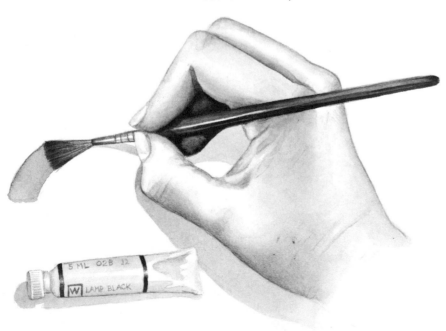

46 Black watercolor was used in this illustration for black-and-white reproduction.

Ink wash is a wet medium, so it must be done on paper that will not buckle from moisture. The best surfaces for a wash are illustration board or stretched watercolor paper. (See the following section on watercolors for instructions on stretching watercolor paper.) If the line drawing has been made on regular drawing paper, an overlay of frosted acetate is the better solution.

To mix the washes, you will need three to five small containers, such as paper cups. There is no need to make more than one-fourth to one-third cup of each.

Use the following formulas for shade gradation in the washes:

- Black ink straight out of the jar for a black wash.
- Cup 1—mix one part ink with two parts water.
- Cup 2—mix one part ink with four parts water.
- Cup 3—mix one part ink with six parts water.
- Cup 4—mix one part ink with eight parts water.
- Cup 5—mix one part ink with ten parts water.

Mix each cup well so there is no concentration of ink at the bottom. These five cups, plus the ink from the jar, will give you six different shades of gray to black wash.

If you would rather start with only three shades of gray, mix the following proportions:

- Cup 1—one part ink with three parts water.
- Cup 2—one part ink with six parts water.
- Cup 3—one part ink with nine parts water.

Now it is up to you to decide where each tone fits in the illustration. Adding tone to a line drawing is something like filling in a coloring book.

Ink washes are similar to watercolors in that both are a transparent medium. This means that the color of the paper (white) is supposed to show through. Do not paint the washes over and over to darken and cover the white unless this really is your intention. Most often you will want to make only one pass over a given area if you have selected the right shade. Leave the paper white with no wash at all where you want it to be the brightest. If you are afraid that you might paint over a small white detail with the wash, cover it with liquid frisket beforehand to protect it.

Liquid frisket can be purchased at an art store, and it works something like rubber cement. It dries in minutes, and an ink wash painted over it will not penetrate. After the wash is dry, rub the frisket gently with your finger to lift it off, and uncover the white detail.

Apply an ink wash with a round-tipped sable brush sized appropriately for what you are painting. It is a good idea to have several paintbrushes on hand so that you do not resort to using a brush that is too small or too large. For detail work, use a round sable brush #0, 1, or 2. For medium-sized areas, a #7 or 8 or larger brush is recommended. Purchase at least one small brush for detail work, one medium-sized brush, and one larger-sized brush for washes.

Practice painting with the washes on scrap paper before you make an illustration. Try to make at least one large, smooth wash in practice.

HOW TO MAKE A SMOOTH WASH

Painting small areas evenly is usually not difficult. But covering a large area smoothly and without streaks requires more skill. The secret is to do the wash all at once, fairly quickly, so that none of the strokes dry before the wash is finished. It should be started on one side and worked to the other as quickly as possible. Never begin at one place, stop, and start somewhere else. The ink on the first area will dry and leave a telltale mark.

Prior planning is essential to finish the wash quickly. First, know exactly where the wash is to go. If it outlines intricate shapes that demand time-consuming precision, consider using liquid frisket to mask out the shape so you can brush with speed. If the ink wash runs to the border of the illustration, consider masking the edges with cloth tape or another gentle tape that will not tear the paper when it is eventually removed. With the four sides masked, a wash can be carried up and over the edges with vigorous strokes, which makes the process go more quickly. If the wash is very wet, you may run the risk of it seeping under the tape, but this is not terrible. It is true that the edges of an illustration should be clean for the presentation, but the quality of the picture should be the most overriding consideration. That is what will be reproduced, and the edges will be photographically cut off. (For more information on illustration presentation, see *Chapter six*.)

This section describes black watercolor as a black-and-white illustration technique and the implementation of the full spectrum of colors. Since this is a wet medium, it calls for a drawing surface that will not buckle from the moisture, such as illustration board, watercolor board, or stretched watercolor paper.

47 Artist: Linda Gist
Client: Gray & Rogers
Title: *Little Jack Horner*
Media: Watercolors and ink dyes
In this illustration, Linda Gist painted with watercolors and dyes on watercolor board. Although the paint is so smooth that it appears to be airbrushed, the artwork is painted by hand. She uses friskets with watercolors, which accounts for some of the crispness between one color and another.
Gist often masks out areas with paper frisket in order to paint the background and larger areas of the illustration with watercolor wash. She prefers to apply the frisket to the fresh board before it is painted so that there is no possibility of picking up parts of the image when the frisket is removed, although sometimes this is not possible and the frisket is applied and removed very carefully.

Even more so than when airbrushing with friskets, it is difficult to keep paint in a watercolor wash from running under the edges of a frisket. Gist has found that the only solution to this problem is to be sure the frisket is sealed, sometimes using rubber cement (on the edges only) to hold it. She says, "If I leave a frisket on overnight, sometimes the moisture in the air causes it to buckle and I have to brush the edges again." Also, the watercolor wash must be applied so that puddles of paint are not pushed under the frisket.

Gist also uses toothbrush spraying, a technique enjoyed by children in bathroom toothbrush fights. The toothbrush is dipped in paint and rubbed with a finger to make, depending on how diluted the paint is, a fine or coarse spray. She uses this in selected areas, protecting the artwork with frisket.

HOW TO STRETCH WATERCOLOR PAPER

Materials Needed
- *Watercolor paper*
- *Paper tape*
- *Drawing board*
- *Sponge*
- *Scrap paper*

There are two types of watercolor paper you can buy: smooth-finished hot-press or coarse-textured cold-press. Choose the one you prefer, and cut the paper to fit within the dimensions of the drawing board. Even if your board is very clean, it is wise to put down a piece of clean scrap paper the size of the watercolor paper first. Center it in the middle, where you will position the watercolor paper.

The paper tape used to hold the paper is the brown package-sealing type sold in a dry roll. Cut four strips, each slightly larger than the sides of the watercolor paper. Saturate a sponge with water, and place it in a dish nearby to wet the tape later.

Pass both sides of the watercolor paper under a faucet to moisten it completely. Let the excess water run off, then lay the wet paper over the scrap paper on the board. Puddles can be dabbed with paper toweling. Wet the strips of paper tape thoroughly by running them under the sponge, gummed side up. Tape the paper to the board, overlapping the watercolor paper ½" to 1". Smooth the tape with the palm of your hand to be sure it has adhered all around and that the paper is secured on four sides.

The paper will take two hours or more to dry. It may look baggy or buckled when you are stretching it, but it will dry perfectly flat if it is held securely by the paper tape. Do not attempt to start work until it has dried.

The paper must be used as is, taped to the drawing board. This will ensure that it consistently dries flat, no matter how soaked it becomes from the watercolors. When the illustration is finished, the paper is cut away close to the tape with a straightedge and an X-acto knife. The design should have been scaled to leave a border around the illustration.

48 Artist: Marta Thoma
Media: Watercolors

TRANSFER OF A ROUGH DRAWING

Before you begin painting with watercolors, you must transfer the plan of a rough drawing onto the stretched, dried watercolor paper or onto watercolor board. Light guidelines are essential for this transparent medium, especially in parts of the illustration that will be light colored or highly transparent. Unless the guidelines are drawn so lightly that you can barely see them, they will show through the paint. Since watercolor board or paper stretched on a drawing board cannot be used on a light table, you will have to use one of the techniques that follow.

- Transfer the drawing using graphite paper (see *Chapter one*). Graphite paper is used like carbon paper, but it transfers a pencil line instead of an ink line. Practice on scrap paper applying the right amount of pressure to create a *very light line*.
- Project a homemade slide (see *Chapter one*) of the rough drawing onto the stretched paper or watercolor board. Trace the image with a hard, sharp pencil, making a light guideline.
- Draw the plan of the rough drawing freehand onto the watercolor paper or board. Use a hard, sharpened pencil to make a light guideline.

BLACK WATERCOLOR TECHNIQUE

Materials Needed
- *Lamp- or ivory-black watercolor in a tube*
- *Round-tipped sable brushes, in assorted sizes, including a #0 or #1 for detail*
- *Stretched watercolor paper or illustration board*

Black-and-white techniques are fundamental skills for illsutration because any illustration which is to be reproduced in a single color is done in black and white. In other words, you would not use colored paints in the artwork for a black-and-white reproduction even though it was going to be shot in black and white. Different colors photograph differently. For example, on black-and-white film the color red will look like a darker shade of gray than the same intensity of the color blue. Hence, the most successful black-and-white reproductions are made from black-and-white originals.

Black watercolor paint is an excellent technique, similar to ink washes but offering more versatility. Because watercolors dry more slowly, they afford the artist more time to render the image. In addition, they can be dampened and lifted off to some degree, even after they have dried, unlike dry ink, which is permanent.

A tube of black paint is preferable to a cake of dried paint, because you will be starting with a bold black, diluting it for lighter shades of gray. Use small containers or a divided plastic palette to mix several shades of gray, from the darkest to a pale watery one. This can be done in the same proportions of paint to water suggested for ink wash (see page 52.

Read the preceding section on ink washes before you continue, because there are many similarities between ink and black watercolor techniques. Both are a transparent medium, and in both the white of the paper should be allowed to show through, except in the very blackest areas. The discussions of transparency, the use of liquid frisket, paintbrush sizes, and achieving uniformity with a large wash all apply equally to black watercolor.

The application of black watercolor should start with the lightest shade of gray and proceed gradually to the darkest ones. There are two rules about letting the paint dry in between shades:

1. If you want a sharp edge between one shade of gray and another, as in a

geometric pattern or a sharp silhouette, the paint of the first—the lighter one—should be allowed to dry before the second is added.

2. If you want a gradation of light to dark, paint a light shade of wash next to a dark shade while both are wet (but not dripping wet—if puddles form, you will lose control over the paints).

Have a tissue or paper towel handy to blot if you have applied a shade that is too dark. You can also bring out highlights in an image by wetting the designated areas and lifting off the color with a piece of absorbent paper.

Illustrations made this way should be photographed through a halftone screen for reproduction. Since they have a delicate quality, they are not recommended for newspapers, where the coarse screen would lose the subtle shades of gray. Watercolors are best suited for reproduction on fairly good paper, but even then, the light tones disappear. To see if all the tones on your illustration are strong enough to be reproduced, look at your artwork through squinted eyes. If some tones disappear, it is proof that they should be strengthened. If nothing disappears, you have nothing to worry about.

THE FULL SPECTRUM OF WATERCOLORS

A transparent medium like watercolor utilizes the white of the paper to create the light values of the illustration. If you have practiced with ink washes and black-and-white watercolor techniques, you already know how to mix paint and water in washes of varying transparency. The color of the wash becomes paler as the paint is diluted with water.

These same principles apply to the other colors of paint, except that you have greater scope and infinite variety. For example, cadmium red mixed with very little water will be a brilliant red, but diluted much more, it will be pink.

White paint is scarcely used at all, and then very sparingly, to touch up small details on a finished illustration. If you mix white watercolor with cadmium red, the result will be an opaque pink different from the transparent pink made from water-diluted red. The opaque pink will look heavier and grayer, and where each pink may look fine by itself, it will look dreadful next to another. This is why it is important to avoid white paint while using transparent watercolors. The other alternative is to work with white throughout, which is gouache, a technique described later in this chapter.

Tubes of watercolors are more convenient than blocks of dried paint because the color is already in liquid form. When you want the color strong and minimally diluted, adding just a little water improves the flow without diminishing the brilliance.

Since watercolors tend to be soft and muted, it is a good idea to aim for strength and precision by including a full spectrum of values, from white to very dark, in the illustration. The white of the paper should sparkle as the lightest, followed by several intermediate values. The darkest values, which are nearly black, but rarely a real black in color illustration, should give the artwork accent, or "punch."

Liquid frisket can be used to protect delicate white areas that are in danger of being washed over. (See the earlier section in this chapter on ink washes for a description of liquid frisket.) It can also be

Materials Needed
• *Stretched watercolor paper or watercolor board*
• *Selection of round-tipped sable paint brushes (minimum recommended: #0 or #1 for detail, #3 and #8 for large washes)*
• *Watercolor paints, preferably packaged in a tube*

Suggested Colors
• *Primary: cadmium yellow, cadmium red, ultramarine blue*
• *Earth: raw umber, burnt sienna, yellow ochre, burnt umber, sepia*
• *Others: hooker's green, manganese blue, violet, prussian green, ivory black*

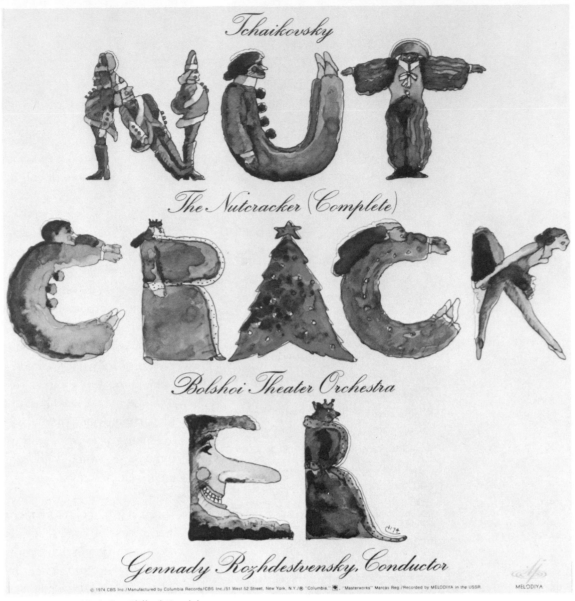

49 Artist: Clifford Condak
Title: *Nutcracker*
Client: Columbia Records

used in experimental ways. For example, frisket splattered on your paper from an old toothbrush will create an image of stars and comets in a night sky if you paint over it with a blue watercolor wash.

EXERCISE IN COLOR MIXING

To become more skillful at mixing and diluting watercolors, try the following exercise. On a piece of watercolor paper, paint color swatches matching the color of the following objects as closely as pos-

sible, which should be readily available:

- Your desk
- A leaf
- Skin
- Hair
- A pair of Levi's jeans
- A branch
- A person's lips

As you are doing the exercise, hold each color swatch right next to the object, touching it if possible, to see if you have matched the color precisely. If it is not right, continue to paint swatches until you devise one that matches.

Next, paint three color swatches for each of the following objects. There should be at least three different colors to pick up in the highlights, in reflected color, or in the shadows of the object:

• Pair of scissors
• Light bulb or light fixture
• Skin
• Pencil
• Hair
• Watch

Once again, hold the color swatches up to the object for careful comparison and repaint until they are accurate.

This exercise serves two purposes: (1) it gives you practice in mixing watercolor washes and making subtle changes in the transparency of the colors, and (2) it gives you practice in seeing and matching colors in nature. Whether or not you intend to use realistic colors in an illustration, this is good training because it increases your skills and control over the medium.

PAINTING THE ARTWORK

Your drawing paper is prepared, the rough drawing has been transferred, and you have practiced with watercolor paints. When you begin to paint, remember these rules, which are similar to those rules for black watercolor technique (described earlier):

1. Leave the white of the paper for white.
2. Paint the lightest colors first, the darker values next, the darkest values last.
3. If two colors are to meet in a sharp line, paint the lighter color and let it dry before painting the next. Two colors should meet with precision; there should be no white of the paper showing through.
4. If colors are to be blended, do so while they are wet. Paint can be manipulated to create a gradation while it is still wet on the paper. Use tissues or paper towels to blot excess water or to lift off color that is too heavy.
5. For specific instructions on painting a large even wash, see the earlier section in this chapter on ink washes. Briefly, the artist must apply the wash in one fast step, moving steadily across the page before the wash can dry. Done all at once in this fashion, the wash should be even and free from streaks. It is important to mix enough wash so that you do not run out in the middle of a large area.

Color Theory

As you start using color, the choices may seem baffling. Every medium from pencils to paints is sold in a large array of colors. How do you know which ones to buy? And then how do you decide what colors will look good together in an illustration?

Later in this section, we will describe some color schemes used by many artists today. Each has rules that lay down guidelines for pleasing color combinations. But before you try the color schemes, it is necessary to understand some color theories and vocabulary.

THE COLOR WHEEL

The best way to begin the study of color theory is to make a color wheel. This will help you visualize the relationships of colors to each other and give you practice mixing colors. (See the color insert, Plate 17, for an illustration of a color wheel.)

To make a color wheel, begin by drawing a large circle, at least 10" in diameter, with pencil on an illustration board. Using a protractor, mark three equidistant points on the circle to divide the 360 degrees into 120-degree sections. You can estimate the three points if you have a good eye. Samples of the three primary colors—red, blue, and yellow—will go on these three points.

Make the samples by painting swatches of color on drawing paper. Cut a piece from each swatch in a circle or square shape and glue the sample into position on the illustration board. This is easier than trying to paint each sample on the board itself because it could take several tries to produce the right color when you begin blending combinations.

The best paint for this exercise is an opaque water-base paint like poster paint or gouache. Acrylics can be used, but some present a problem because they are mixed with a gel medium that makes them slightly transparent. A touch of white will make them more opaque.

Use the primary colors to make all the others in the wheel. Red, blue, and yellow are called "primary" because they are the ingredients of all the colors found in nature. In theory, if the primaries you begin with are very pure, you should produce equally pure results when you mix them. The problem is that the pigments in paint are not flawless like the colors in the light spectrum, and you may find that they do not produce pure rainbow colors when they are combined. That is why most artists find it necessary to purchase secondary colors in an art

medium. However, for the purpose of this exercise and learning how to mix paints, it is best to work with the three primaries. The recommended paints are cadmium yellow light, ultramarine blue, and cadmium red medium (which tends to be slightly yellow and needs some crimson).

When you have the primary colors in place on the color wheel, the next step is to paint samples of secondary colors, which will be positioned in between them. Secondary colors are produced by combining primary colors. For example, red and blue make violet, yellow and blue produce green, and yellow and red make orange. The green, violet, and orange will be mounted between the colors from which they were made. Leave room between the primary and secondary samples for six more—the tertiary colors. Tertiary colors are made by mixing each primary color with its neighboring secondary colors. The results are red-violet, blue-violet, blue-green, yellow-green, red-orange, and yellow-orange. The completed wheel will look like a color clock composed of twelve samples.

A SUMMARY OF BASIC COLORS

Primary colors: Red, yellow, and blue are called "primary" because they are the ingredients of all the other colors.

Secondary colors: Orange, green, and violet are made by mixing pairs of primary colors.

Tertiary colors: Red-violet, blue-violet, blue-green, yellow-orange, red-orange, and yellow-green are produced by mixing primary colors with neighboring tertiary colors. Names of tertiary colors are hyphenated words which list the primary color first, followed by the neighboring secondary color.

COLOR TERMINOLOGY

Complementary Colors. After you have made a color wheel, it will be easy to understand the definition of complementary colors because complementaries are colors located directly across the wheel from each other. Examples of complementary color pairs are red and green, violet and yellow, orange and blue, blue-green and red-orange.

Why are these colors called complementary? In the light spectrum, complementaries complete each other to make the combination of all colors, white. In painting, complementary colors neutralize each other when they are mixed to produce a gray or brown similar to the color that results from combining all of the primary colors. Used together in art work, complementary colors create visual tension, but they can be used to make pleasing color schemes, as discussed later in this chapter.

Hue. The word *hue* is used interchangeably with the word *color.* It refers to various locations on the light spectrum that are identified as violet, blue, green, yellow, orange, red, and hues in between. Primary, secondary, and tertiary colors are all hues.

COLOR VALUES

The lightness or darkness of a hue determines its value. Some colors are naturally darker in value than others; for example, violet is dark in value and yellow is light.

Color values change as white or black is mixed with a hue. With the addition of black, a color becomes darker in value. When white is added, the color value is lightened. For example, by mixing red paint with white, the color pink is produced, a light value of the color red.

The terms used to describe values are *light, medium-light, medium, medium-dark,* and *dark.* Colors that have been deepened in value by the addition of black are "shades" of the color. Colors mixed with white are referred to as "tints."

To practice mixing color values, try the following exercises.

Exercise 1. Choose a hue from the color wheel and mix it with the following proportions of black and white:

- Three-fourths part color with one-fourth white.
- One-half part color with one-half part white.
- One-fourth part color with three-fourths part white.
- Nine-tenths part color with one-tenth part black.
- Seven-eighths part color with one-eighth part black.
- Three-fourths part color with one-fourth part black.

Estimate the amounts, measuring them in dabs of paint from your brush. The suggested portions of black are small because black affects value change quickly.

Paint a sample swatch of each color value suggested above, as well as the original color. Cut a 2″ square out of each swatch, and glue them all together in a progression of values from lightest to darkest.

Exercise 2.   This exercise will add an inner and an outer wheel of dark and light color values to your original color wheel.

• To make the inner wheel, mix each color on the wheel with one-half part color and one-half part white.
• For the outer wheel, mix each color with four-fifths part color and one-fifth part black.

Paint the color values as swatches on drawing paper, and cut out a circular or square sample of the color as you did for the original color wheel. Mount the values of the same hue next to each other. You should have three values of each hue around the wheel.

COLOR INTENSITY

Color intensity refers to the brilliance or purity of a color. A color of high intensity contains no black, gray, white, or other color that might dull its effect. A low-intensity color is one that is no longer pure because it has been mixed with a neutralizing color such as gray. Degrees of color intensity are described as *high, medium-high, medium, medium-low,* and *low.*

WARM & COOL COLORS

On one side of the color wheel are the hues referred to as "warm"—yellow, orange, red, and their neighboring tertiary colors. On the other side are the "cool" colors—blue, green, and their neighboring tertiaries.

The warm and cool terminology derives from the association of colors with images found in nature. Yellow, orange, and red suggest sunlight, heat, fire, and blood, images which range in temperature from warm to hot and imply liveliness and aggression. Blue and green are associated in nature with water and foliage, which are cool, restful images.

COLOR ASSOCIATIONS

The way that cool and warm colors are "felt" is an example of how we respond tactually and emotionally to colors. Following are the basic colors and the emotional responses they elicit from the viewer, described by Faber Birren in *Color Psychology & Color Therapy* (Secaucus, NJ: Citadel Press, 1978, adapted with permission of the publisher).

The Significance of Red.   Red is perhaps the most dominant and dynamic of colors. It has even been found to increase hormonal and sexual activity and heal wounds! In its action upon the human organism, red tends to disturb the equilibrium of the body. It will raise blood pressure and pulse rate.

Under practical situations, however, pure red can seldom be used; the full hue is too imperious and has too strong an after-image. Brilliant red commands human attention (hence, stop lights and fire engines), but a high frequency of color blindness among men limits its usefulness. Modified forms of red –rose, maroon, and pink are beautiful, expressive, universally appealing, and deeply emotional.

Variations of Orange.   Orange has qualities similar to red. It is not generally popular in its pure form, but it is highly pleasing in tints (peach, salmon) and shades (brown).

Yellow. Yellow is said to affect human metabolism favorably. Its high visibility serves many purposes in safety (increasing numbers of fire engines are yellow instead of red). The hue is sharply focused by the eye, cheerful, and incandescent in appearance. Yellow tends to appear brighter than white.

Greens in General. Yellow-green is neutral from the physiological standpoint. Greens and blue-greens, however, tend to reduce nervous and muscular tension. Psychologically, green represents a withdrawal from stimulus.

Bluish greens are pleasing, as is peach, and, indeed, the two hues beautifully enhance each other.

Significance of Blue. The qualities in blue produce the exact antithesis of the effects of red. In its action upon the human organism, blue lowers blood pressure and pulse rate. Because it has a naturally low saturation, blue can be used in almost any form—light, dark, pure, grayish. As it is visually primary, however, it tends to be bleak if applied in too large an area.

Restful and sedate, blue is associated with dim light and is a general favorite throughout the world.

Purple, Gray, White, and Black. Since purple is a blend of red and blue, the two extremes of the spectrum, it is more or less biologically neutral. It is not suitable for large areas because it disturbs the focus of the eye, but of all the hues, purple seems to be dominantly aesthetic in its appeal.

White is the perfectly balanced color, clear and natural in its influence. Black is negative; gray is passive. All three are emotionally neutral.

COLOR SCHEMES

For hundreds of years, artists and color theorists have tried to devise color systems to produce pleasing color combinations. The most widely recognized of the many color scheme experiments are the monochromatic, analogous, and complementary schemes.

As you read these descriptions, keep in mind that a color scheme is defined by the *predominant hues* in the artwork. Other colors may be included as long as they are subtle or otherwise unobtrusive in the overall scheme.

Monochromatic Color Scheme. As the name suggests, a monochromatic color scheme is composed of only one color. Variation is created by changing the value of the color. A blue monochromatic scheme might consist of such shades and tints of blue as navy blue, pure blue, gray-blue, pale blue, and so on. A red-orange monochromatic color scheme might feature the predominant hue blended with black, white, or gray, to appear as dark brown, red-brown, red-orange, peach, and pale pink.

A monochromatic color scheme can be conceived as a single color wash on top of a black-and-white design. Waterproof ink or acrylic washes work well for this technique.

The predominant color of a monochromatic color scheme will pronounce the mood of the artwork. Refer to the preceding paragraphs on color associations.

Analogous Color Scheme. An analogous color scheme comprises the secondary and tertiary hues adjacent to a primary color or the hues between one primary color and another. These can be applied in a variety of values and intensities, but an analogous color scheme does not extend beyond the bounds of two primary colors.

Such a scheme worked around yellow might include green-yellow, yellow, yellow-orange, and orange. In this example, yellow is the common denominator among the colors. A sense of harmony and unity is created in an analogous color scheme because there is always one primary color which is the common denominator.

Any number of colors can be used, as long as they are within the bounds of two primary colors. An extensive color scheme worked around yellow could range from red-orange, orange, and yellow-orange to yellow, yellow-green, and blue-green.

Below are more examples of analogous color schemes. The possibilities are endless, and colors may be applied in varying values and intensities.

- Violet, blue-violet, blue, and blue-green
- Red-violet, violet, blue-violet, and blue
- Blue-green, green, yellow-green, yellow, and yellow-orange

Complementary Color Schemes.   There are three important complementary color schemes—the basic complementary scheme, the double complementary scheme, and the split complementary scheme.

The *basic complementary color scheme* is predominantly composed of two complementary colors, hues located directly opposite each other on the color wheel such as red and green, yellow and violet, orange and blue. In contrast to monochromatic and analogous color schemes, which are based on colors similar to each other, complementary schemes appeal because their difference or opposition creates an interesting tension.

Complementary schemes are often most effective when one color is a high intensity and its complementary is subdued. For example, a bright green looks good with pink, a subdued version of red. This reduces the tension between the two colors while retaining the appealing combination of colors.

A *double complementary color scheme* is predominantly made up of two colors and their complementaries. Such a scheme might include red, green, violet, and yellow. Here again, varying the intensities and values of the colors makes the combinations more harmonious. For example, a pleasing color scheme might include brilliant reds and violets with more subdued green and yellow. There are many possible color combinations in a double complementary color scheme.

A *split complementary color scheme* is composed of a color and the two hues that flank each side of its complementary color. For example, the color scheme might be red, blue-green, and yellow-green; blue-green and yellow-green are located on either side of green, the complementary of red. The term "split complementary" refers to the divided function of the complementary color.

Other examples of split complementary color combinations include:

- Yellow with red-violet and blue-violet

- Blue with yellow-orange and red-orange
- Violet with yellow-green and yellow-orange
- Orange with blue-green and blue-violet
- Red-violet with green and yellow

Planning a Color Scheme. Construction paper can be useful for planning a color scheme. Try cutting out samples of colored paper and using them in a mock-up design for an illustration. This is a quick way to see how the colors you will eventually paint look together. With a wide variety of paper colors, you can try several color combinations, then choose the best one for your artwork.

Suggested Exercises

1. Make a color wheel using the method described in this section. Label the primary, secondary, and tertiary colors.
2. Do the two exercises recommended for learning color values.
3. Analyze a color illustration in this book for the following.
   - Is there a color scheme in the artwork?
   - What are the predominant hues?
   - Are there varying values and intensities of colors? Describe them.
   - What mood do the colors create?
4. Use the construction paper method to preplan a color illustration. Try at least two different color schemes, and explain in writing your reasons for choosing the final color scheme.

Colored Inks

Most of the watercolor techniques described previously are applicable to colored inks because they have similar qualities; both are a transparent medium and diluted with water. The difference is that inks dry more quickly than watercolors and are permanent. For this reason, they are less suited to modeling images and are better for application as a flat wash. The exception to this is when colored inks are used in an airbrush. As a wash or with subtle manipulations of tone, colored inks can be applied in fine detail to make beautiful illustrations.

Inks are available in more brilliant colors than watercolors. Indeed, some of them have a "psychedelic" quality of brightness. However, they are not especially strong colors, since they are already diluted to a runny consistency. Deepen ink colors on your artwork by applying more than one coat, allowing each coat to dry before adding the next.

Colored inks and watercolors are compatible techniques when used together. Each has its own outstanding qualities.

- Watercolors—easier to model or make gradations
- Colored inks—bright colors, good consistency for airbrushing right out of the jar

You may wish to use both in an illustration by painting most of the artwork in watercolor, then airbrushing colored inks on top for the finish.

50 Artist: Marta Thoma
Media: Colored inks

51 Artist: Marta Thoma
Media: Colored inks

50

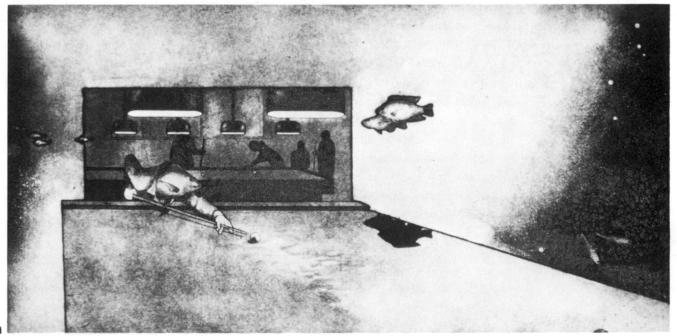

51

Painting with Gouache

Gouache paints are watercolors that are opaque instead of transparent. They cover the drawing surface so that the paper or board beneath does not show through and become an element of the design. Similar to tempera paints in texture and appearance, they tend to be more expensive because they are usually better quality, longer-lasting pigments. Gouache can be purchased at an art store or made by mixing transparent watercolors with white gouache paint.

This medium does not blend easily or naturally and is best suited for areas of flat color. If you do wish to model or blend colors, it must be done quickly, while the paint is still wet.

One interesting way to work with gouache is to paint on colored paper or hand-colored watercolor board. If a medium-tone drawing surface is used, white gouache will stand out as highlights and a darker paint can be used to define shadows and distinguish images.

Colored Pencils

Colored pencils are excellent for making soft, subtly colored illustrations. They can be used alone or in combination with other techniques, such as watercolors or acrylics. Choose an artist brand of colored pencils to be sure that they are good quality. There are two different types: one is water-soluble, and the other is not. Either type is excellent for drawing, but if you want to experiment by making washes from the pencil drawing, choose a kind that is water-soluble.

Unless you are using colored pencils with a wet medium, they are considered a dry technique, so they can be used on drawing paper, drawing board, or almost any good quality drawing surface. A rough drawing can be transferred to the drawing surface by any of the following methods (all described in *Chapter one*):

1. Use a light table if you are using drawing paper.
2. Use graphite paper.
3. Project a homemade slide of the rough drawing to trace.

Colored pencils are a transparent medium, which makes it imperative to transfer the guidelines of the rough drawing *very lightly*. The rough drawing transfer is perfect if it is barely visible.

DRAWING TECHNIQUES

Colored pencils can be applied in a technique that is like a modified crosshatch. Crosshatching with colored pencils is similar to the technique described in *Chapter two*, except that the pencil is held with the point resting on its side. In this way, no lines are made and a smooth tone is achieved. By drawing in this way and moving in many directions—horizontally, vertically, and diagonally—you can build up even color without lines or streaks. Try to keep a uniform pressure on the pencil as you cross back and forth.

Gradations are made by increasing and decreasing the density of the shading. Practice making a smooth gradation on a test strip 2″ × 6″. Start with the darkest shade of a color by densely crosshatching; then gradually decrease the crosshatching for paler values, until the shading is nearly

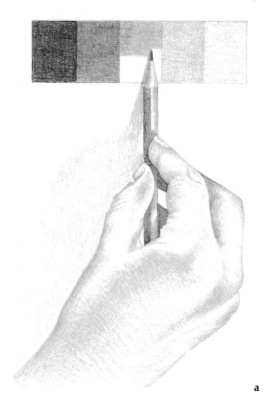

a

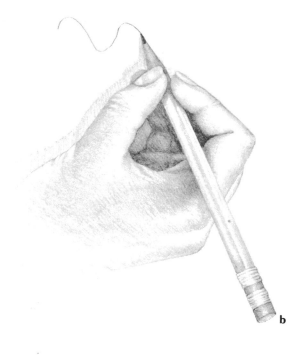

b

52 Artist: Marta Thoma
Media: Pencils

53a & b Drawing techniques

invisible. I ry to encompass several intermediate values from dark to light in the test strip.

In the lighter values of color on the test strip, you will notice that the colored pencil is transparent, like a "glaze" on top of the paper, which permits the white to show through. Applying a second color on top of the first—let's say red over blue—is called a "glazing technique." Colors can be combined in this way to make a third color: for example, blue glazed on top of red will give the illusion of purple. This is not to suggest that you use only primary colors to make others. It is best to use many different colored pencils and to combine them to make even more interesting, vibrant hues.

Of course, colored pencils are also adapted to all the line techniques described in *Chapter two,* such as

stippling, texturing, and mechanical crosshatching. Using several colors on top of one another in these techniques will generate interesting effects.

WITH WATERCOLORS OR ACRYLIC PAINTS

Colored pencils are good for adding small details and glazes of color on top of watercolors and acrylic paints. When water-soluble pencils are used, they can be moistened to blend in with the other mediums. However, if you are skilled at drawing smooth tones with colored pencil, you will be able to do it with dry pencils.

Colored pencils over flat acrylic colors is a good-looking technique for the comprehensive drawing, which is often required prior to the final art for detailed

54

54 Artist: Edward Wong-Ligda
Media: Carbon pencils on paper
This drawing was made with carbon pencils of different grades, from HB to 3B, on Strathmore paper. Wong-Ligda says, "These pencils give me a wide range of darks and lights. With the hard pencils, I can make think controlled lines and with the softer pencils I can draw heavy, more accentuated lines. I use many other media for my artwork, but this is my favorite."

His favorite subject is people, because, "People interest me more than anything else. The subtle curves and constantly changing expressions of people create an exciting challenge." Wong-Ligda draws from life or from Polaroid shots of a model. He has shown unswerving dedication to becoming a portrait artist. He says, "In college I took innumerable life drawing, fashion illustration, and portrait classes. I also copied Degas, Manet, Ingres, Hopper, and others out of books. Since college, I have drawn from a live model at least once a week to keep in practice."

55 Artist: Teresa Fasolino
Client: *Ms. Magazine*
Art Director: Bea Feitler
Media: Acrylic paints and collage on canvas
This scene created by Teresa Fasolino is simultaneously realistic and unrealistic. The illustration is made up of incongruous images; a cafe sign on what appears to be a large bedroom window, a cotton field in the background, which belongs to neither scene. Does the scene in the picture window symbolize the figure's thoughts or dreams? The images provoke such questions. Yet the images are combined subtly so that they look natural (and believable) together.

work such as oil paintings or airbrushed illustrations. The pencil-acrylic method is reasonably fast in comparison to the more time-consuming techniques, and it can indicate the color and detail of the final artwork.

STEPS TO MAKE A COLOR COMPREHENSIVE

1. Apply acrylic paints to define the general design and composition of the artwork. If, for example, the artwork is a landscape with green hills, a small town, and a blue sky, each of the three elements should be indicated with a separate color. (For details on how to mix and apply acrylic paints, see the next section.)

2. After the paint is dry, define the details and make shading in the artwork with colored pencils. The town buildings could be given shadows and definition; the hills could be shaded; the sky could be given white clouds; and so on.

Acrylic Paints

Materials Needed
- *Illustration board or a drawing surface such as masonite or stretched canvas.*
- *A selection of round and flat sable brushes, ranging from small to large*
- *Acrylic paints*

Suggested Colors
- *Primary: cadmium yellow, cadmium red, ultramarine blue*
- *Earth: raw umber, yellow ochre, burnt sienna, burnt umber*
- *Others: hooker's green, thalo blue, thalo crimson, titanic white, blue-green, ivory black*

Acrylics are versatile paints that can be used as a transparent or opaque medium. They can be sprayed out of an airbrush, painted in flat colors, applied in glazes for a modeled effect, or mixed with a drying retardant and used like oil paints. Their flexibility and brilliant colors make them an excellent medium for illustration.

56

57

56 Artist: Wilson McLean
Client: *Penthouse*
Media: Acrylics on canvas

57 Artist: Kim Thoman
Media: Acrylics on canvas

MATERIALS

Since acrylics are a wet medium, they must be used on a surface that will not buckle. The most practical choice is probably illustration board, but masonite or stretched canvas will work.

1. Illustration board is available in hot or cold press; the choice is up to you. Do not use a pebbly board.
2. Masonite can be purchased at a hardware store. It is naturally brown with one rough and one smooth side. The smooth side should be covered with a few coats of white gesso, diluted in the proportions of two-thirds gesso to one-third water. Paint the gesso on with a wide brush, letting it dry and sanding between coats. This will be your drawing surface. The rough side of the masonite should also be given a coat of gesso to prevent the board from buckling.
3. Ready-made stretched canvas sold in art stores is generally poor quality, rough textured, and badly put together. Stretch your own canvas with a wooden stretcher-bar kit or homemade stretcher bars. A piece of one-quarter-inch round edging should be nailed to all four sides of the stretcher bars. Use a jeweler's saw to cut the edging at right angles for a perfect fit. Stretch a piece of unprimed canvas on top of the bars by stapling one side, then pulling the opposite side tight, and stapling it. Apply several coats of gesso to the stretched canvas, sanding between coats for a smooth painting surface. For more details on do-it-yourself canvas preparation, consult an artist materials handbook at the library or bookstore.

Paintbrushes used for acrylics must be given special care if they are to last.

Acrylic paint dries quickly, and it is very difficult, if not impossible, to remove it from the brush once it has dried. Keep a jar of water nearby at all times to hold the paintbrush when it is not in use. Wash the brush with a gentle detergent when you have finished painting for the day.

Acrylics are sold in jars or in tubes. The tube paint tends to have more gel than the paint in the jar, and the difference can be annoying if you are trying to paint flat colors. The gel makes the tube paint more transparent and better suited for transparent techniques like glazing.

When you are ready to begin painting, transfer the design of a rough drawing by using one of the techniques listed below. Keep in mind that the guidelines must be light enough to be obscured by whatever technique you are using. They should be almost invisible if you are going to use a transparent glazing technique.

1. Transfer the drawing using graphite paper (see *Chapter one* for details). The graphite paper is used like carbon paper, except that a pencil line is transferred instead of an ink line.
2. Project a homemade slide of the rough drawing onto the drawing surface (see *Chapter one* for details). Trace the image with a sharp pencil.
3. Draw the plan of the rough drawing onto the drawing surface freehand.

PAINTING TECHNIQUES

Painting Flat Colors. To cover a flat, even area with acrylics, begin by mixing the paints with a small amount of water to make them flow smoothly. Always mix enough color so that you do not have to stop painting to mix more. For a smooth, opaque look, it is best to apply more than one coat, letting the paint dry between applications.

Some colors have more covering ability than others. Almost all acrylic paints fresh out of the jar or tube will be more opaque and cover the surface more evenly if they are mixed with a very small amount of white paint.

Unlike watercolors, acrylics are permanent and waterproof once they have dried. Since they dry quickly to a firm plastic surface, they cannot be reworked, but they can easily be painted over. A mistake can be covered up as soon as it is dry. If you plan to make a radical color change, from navy to yellow, for example, paint one or more coats of white on top of the navy before substituting the yellow.

Blending Colors.   There are four methods of blending colors with acrylic paints:

1. Blending fast and furiously before the paint can dry.
2. Mixing a drying retardant with the paint (which gives you more time to blend).
3. Using a transparent glazing technique.
4. Spraying the acrylics with an airbrush (described later in this chapter).

Art stores sell a retardant gel that combines with acrylic paints to slow down the drying time. The gel also changes the consistency of the paint somewhat, making it gooier. The more gel added to the paint, the slower it will dry, and the better chance you will have to blend the colors carefully.

Acrylics can be applied in a transparent glazing technique which blends colors by superimposing them on one another. A great deal of control is required in this technique, as forms are built up layer by layer. Done with skill, this method can render images as realistic as a photograph.

For glazing, the acrylic paints are thinned with water to make washes, the way watercolors are prepared for washes. The difference between the two is that the acrylic wash dries to form a permanent film. Once it has dried, another film, or glaze, of a second color can be applied over it. The two colors do not mix, but rest on top of each other like layers of colored glass to produce a third color.

58 Artist: Bill Chambers
Art Director: Bill Chambers
Media: Acrylic paints

Start with glazes of light value and gradually build up tone with repeated overlays of color. In the areas where the illustration should be lightest, only one or two glazes should be needed. More should be applied for the middle values, and several will be necessary to create the deep colors and tones of the illustration.

How do you know what colors will look like as they are glazed over each other?

Make a color test sheet to see what new colors you can make, noting the color of the paints used to make them.

White acrylic paint can also be used as a glaze. The glare from a light bulb can be suggested with a white glaze radiating from the bulb. The glaze should be heavy nearest the bulb, and gradually grow lighter with increasing distance from the light bulb.

Oil Paints

Oil paints are excellent for blending colors and rendering three-dimensional images. Well-known for these qualities, they are also renowned as slow drying and,

therefore, as an impractical medium for illustration. Actually, oils can be conveniently used for illustrating if they are applied as a thin surface which will take no more than two days to dry. Oils can be painted over acrylic paints, but the reverse is not true. Acrylics should not be painted on top of oil paints.

MATERIALS

Oil paints require a drawing surface that has been prepared with a coat of gesso. If you are planning to paint on illustration board, choose a heavy stock that will not buckle from the gesso application and paint the back side with one coat of gesso to equalize the pull on the two sides.

Oil paints can be applied on top of acrylics painted on any surface. The

59 Artist: Marta Thoma
Media: Oil paints

Materials Needed
- *Illustration board, masonite, or stretched canvas*
- *Selection of round and flat sable brushes, ranging from small to large*
- *Paint thinner such as turpentine*
- *Oil paints*
- *Palette or mixing surface*

Suggested Colors
- *Primaries: cadmium yellow, cadmium red, ultramarine or windsor blue*
- *Earth: raw umber, yellow ochre, burnt sienna, burnt umber*
- *Others: veridian green, mauve (violet), indigo, zinc or titanic white, ivory black*

60 Artist: Marta Thoma
Title: *Michael Eating an Orange*
Media: Oil paints

acrylic paints act as a natural "ground" for the oil paints, since they are waterproof and oil resistant, so the oil does not seep into them.

If you wish to paint on masonite or stretched canvas, see the preceding section on acrylic paints for instructions on preparing both of these drawing surfaces.

When you think of oil paints, you probably envision mixing a concoction of linseed oil, varnish, and turpentine to mix with the paints. However, the extra oil and

varnish are not necessary, especially for illustration purposes. Oil paints already contain linseed oil, and adding more only adds to the amount of time it will take the paints to dry. The purpose of adding varnish is to give a glossy finish, which is unnecessary. All you really need is turpentine or a turpentine substitute to thin the paint and wash your brushes.

Brushes for oils should be purchased in many sizes and cared for so they last. When you have finished painting, wash first your paintbrushes with turpentine, then with a mild detergent. Treat the hairs of the brushes gently so they do not bend or break off.

When you are ready to begin painting, transfer a rough drawing onto the painting surface with one of these techniques:

1. Use graphite paper (see *Chapter one* for details).
2. Project and trace a homemade slide of the rough drawing (see *Chapter one* for details).
3. Draw the rough drawing design carefully freehand.

PAINTING TECHNIQUES

Oil paints should be applied in a thin layer if they are to dry in a reasonable length of time. Never make an illustration with a thick impasto of paint. You will not be able to transport it or send it through the mail to a client until it dries, which may be a few months to a year! Remember that linseed oil also inhibits the drying process.

The paints should be applied in a thin layer, but enough to cover the drawing surface. This amount will take several hours to dry, during which time you can be blending colors and rendering the image.

To begin, start in one section of the painting and paint in the general color. Then begin blending the colors and smoothing the paint. Add small amounts of light paint to make highlights, and add darker tones to deepen shadows. Integrate these with the other colors to make them look natural. As one section of the painting takes shape, move on to other areas and apply the paint in the same manner.

Suppose you make a mistake and want to change a color? Wipe off as much paint as possible with a rag, let the area dry for a few hours, and paint over the mistake. Do not try to paint on top of wet paint with another color or you will make a muddy mess. Do not wait for a day or two for the paint to dry before painting over it; not only will this take time, but the second layer of paint will take even more time to dry. The best solution is to wipe the mistake off, using a little turpentine if necessary.

Oil paints can be put over acrylics using the same technique described above, perhaps to paint details in the illustration. The two paints will look so similar that it will be impossible to tell them apart. Here also a thin coat is necessary for quick drying.

Suggested Exercises

Prepare a hypothetical illustration assignment for each of the techniques described. Assign yourself, or the class, a subject topic and dimensions for each assignment. Make thumbnail sketches and a rough drawing for the assignments. Transfer the rough drawings onto the drawing surfaces for the final artwork by the method recommended for each medium.

TECHNIQUES TO TRY

1. Ink washes on top of a simple line illustration
2. Transparent watercolors

3. Black watercolor technique
4. Colored inks
5. Gouache
6. Colored pencils
7. Colored pencils and acrylic paints

8. Acrylic paints in flat colors
9. Acrylic paints blended, opaque
10. Acrylic paints as glazes
11. Oil paints
12. Oil paints on top of acrylics

The Airbrushed Illustration

WHY THE ENTHUSIASM FOR AIRBRUSHING?

The airbrush can quickly create effects that are difficult to achieve with any other technique. The fine spray produces a soft texture without paint strokes or drawing marks to interrupt the surface. This flawless texture and the ease of manipulating tones subtly are ideal for illustrating.

Colors can be blended so gradually that it is hard to tell where one ends and another begins. Consider, for example, a scene at sunset. The gold color from the sun setting on the horizon blends into a red, which blends into the blue of the early evening sky. An airbrush could easily synthesize this sunset with colored paint.

In contrast to these sensual qualities, an airbrush can also be characterized as

61

mechanical and exacting unlike other drawing or painterly illustration techniques. By spraying over stencils, sharp, hard-edged images are created.

All of these contrasting qualities—sensual, subtle textures combined with crisp, precise forms—lend themselves to the perfection and attention to detail of the realistic and surrealistic styles of illustration. There are endless possibilities for the use of the airbrush in many other styles as well.

62

63

61 Artist: Richard Leech
Client: Yamaha
Media: Airbrushed watercolors and pencil
To make a detailed Yamaha bike illustration, Richard Leech begins with a rough pencil drawing. Yamaha provides him with photos of the bike, as well as the bike itself, to work from. Drawing from a combination of these, Leech perfects the sketch using rulers and drafting templates. When the rough drawing has been approved, Leech prepares to make the final artwork. To begin, he has the rough drawing photographed, printed on semiglossy photographic paper, and dry-mounted on board. The drawing is photographed in continuous tone so that it appears as a soft pencil-like line, rather than a harsh black line. Leech also masks out the negative so that no unwanted tone will print on the white background.

To spray the artwork, Leech prefers a Thayer and Chandler airbrush because of its versatility. This model can spray very fine areas, as well as large ones. To mask out elements while he is airbrushing, Leech has devised an original technique that works well as frisket paper on the photographic surface. He paints transparent rubber cement on plastic wrap. When it dries it forms a film that he picks up and rubs down on the drawing.

Leech also airbrushes Pelikan opaque watercolors on a semigloss surface because this enables him to mop up areas that are unsatisfactory. He says, "I don't think I've done a job yet where I haven't had to wipe something off." Although most of the artwork is airbrushed, the smallest details, like screw heads and springs, are painted freehand with a fine brush.

62, 63, 64 Stages of the airbrushed art.
65 The finished artwork. The air gun works by pressing down on the metal button with your forefinger and slowly pulling the button toward the hand. (*Note:* Left-handed airbrushes are available from some dealers. The paint bowl is attached to the opposite side so that you can see the artwork as you are spraying.)

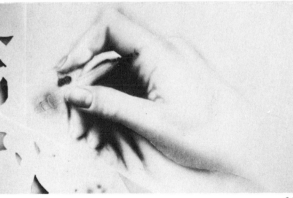
64

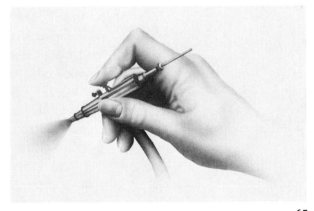
65

THE AIRBRUSH

If you have never seen an airbrush, imagine a miniature spray gun of the house-painting variety, small enough to fit in your hand, and you have the idea. The airbrush is connected by a long hose to an air compressor, a small engine that pumps air at an even rate.

An understanding of the mechanics of the airbrush will help you achieve the best results. You will want to familiarize yourself with the manual for your particular airbrush so that you understand the working parts. At times, you will need to dismantle parts of the gun to clean it. In the process, you will quickly learn how the parts fit together.

Let us consider some of the major parts of the airbrush that are standard on all models and perform the most important functions in its operation: the paint container, the spray adjusting controls, and the airbrush tip.

The paint container is a cup or jar which sits on top of or alongside the airbrush shaft. It can be unscrewed and removed for easy cleaning. The consistency of the paint is crucial in airbrushing; it must flow easily from the container without clogging, so it cannot be too thick or too thin. The correct consistency for a small airbrush is like that of a bottle of ink (assuming a small airbrush is appropriate for an illustrator). The paint itself may be any one of several mediums—watercolors, acrylic paints, and inks are all water-soluble and can be diluted to a good spraying consistency. Ink may be further thinned with water for a fine spray.

If the paint is too thick, it can stop up the container and the airbrush tip, which may result in coarse or irregular spraying, large blobs of paint, or no spray at all. If the paint is too thin, the color will be pastel and diluted. If you want a more intense color, either spray several coats or thicken the paint. Be careful not to spray puddles in an effort to intensify the color.

The paint container on the airbrush is small, and if there is no lid it should be filled only to the halfway point to avoid accidental spillage. This should cause no problem, as you can pre-mix your paint and keep it conveniently nearby to refill the cup as needed.

In the center of the airbrush shaft is a control button. The best position for holding the airbrush is with your first finger on this button, and your thumb and remaining three fingers holding onto the shaft leading to the hose.

The control button has two actions, down and back and forth. Pressing it down when the compressor is running will start the spray. The downward motion simply turns the brush on. To adjust the fineness of the spray, you press the control button back and forth along the airbrush shaft, while keeping it pressed down. Pressing the button forward toward the airbrush tip will press the needle inside the shaft forward, which permits less paint to escape and produces the finest spray. This is the best position for spraying details. As you pull the button in the opposite direction, the needle is pulled back, and the spray becomes broader. This is a good position for spraying large areas. Adjusting the controls may feel awkward at first, but with practice they will become second nature.

The tip of the airbrush should be closely watched because this area, where the paint sprays out, can easily be plugged up by pieces of dried paint or paint that is too thick. If you plan to spray for some time, check the tip at 20-minute intervals to be sure it is clean and free from paint buildup. It is easily removed for cleaning.

The hose which connects the airbrush to the compressor should be long and light enough to allow you to handle the airbrush with ease since you may move around, but the compressor is stationary. The compressor should put out 30 pounds of pressure for an artist-style airbrush. (You can buy a small compressor designed to put out this amount of pressure.) If you have a more powerful one, you will need to adjust the release valve to 30 pounds, because a higher rate will damage your airbrush.

Even at the correct pressure, the compressor will heat up if it is run for a long period of time. Give the engine a rest now and again to let it cool. It is basically a durable machine and should give you years of wear.

HOW TO CHOOSE AN AIRBRUSH

Airbrushes come in different sizes, and your selection will be based on the breadth of the spray you need. However, every size is versatile within a certain range. A very-fine airbrush can make a broad spray, but that spray will not be as broad as one from a larger-size gun. Conversely, the larger airbrush can adjust to a fine spray, but not as fine as that of the smaller airbrush. Except for work that will be exceedingly large, the finest-size airbrush is best for illustrating.

A simple, versatile airbrush is your best bet. And a simple cup to hold the paint is more convenient in the long run than a jar with a lid once you get used to handlng the airbrush.

Some brands have interchangeable needles and tips for changing the size of the spray. These are unnecessary, however, if your airbrush can produce very fine spray and can be adjusted with finger controls to a broader spray.

Be sure to choose an airbrush that is easy to clean! Here again, if the parts are simple, you have the advantage of minimal cleaning. Naturally it will have to be cleaned before you use it, now and then as you are spraying and when you have finished. Good cleaning habits are essential for good airbrushing. Remember this, and make it easy on yourself when you choose one.

GETTING READY

Before you begin to airbrush, you will need to gather and/or prepare the items discussed below.

Newspaper and Scrap Paper. Newspapers will protect your table top and allow you to work freely. Scrap paper is convenient for practice spraying and for some of the techniques that will be described later.

Broad-mouthed Containers (2). Both should be half-filled with cool water. Add a dash of detergent to one for cleansing the airbrush when it is clogged and for the final cleaning of the day. The clear water is used to flush the airbrush when you change from one color to another. To flush it, you can either lower it into the water container so that water fills the paint cup or turn it on underwater, where it will bubble instead of spray. Hold it under for 5 to 20 seconds, depending on how much flushing is needed.

66

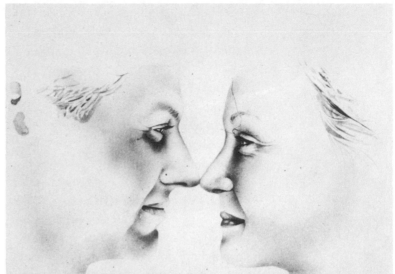

66 Artwork partially airbrushed.

67 Artist: Marta Thoma
Client: Benjamin/Cummings Publishing Company
Media: Airbrushed and hand-painted watercolors
Title: Artwork of man and woman profiles. Reprinted by permission from Barbara J. Combs, Dianne R. Hales, and Brian K. Williams, *An Invitation to Health: Your Personal Responsibility* (Menlo Park, Calif.: The Benjamin/Cummings Publishing Company, 1980, pp. 140–141.

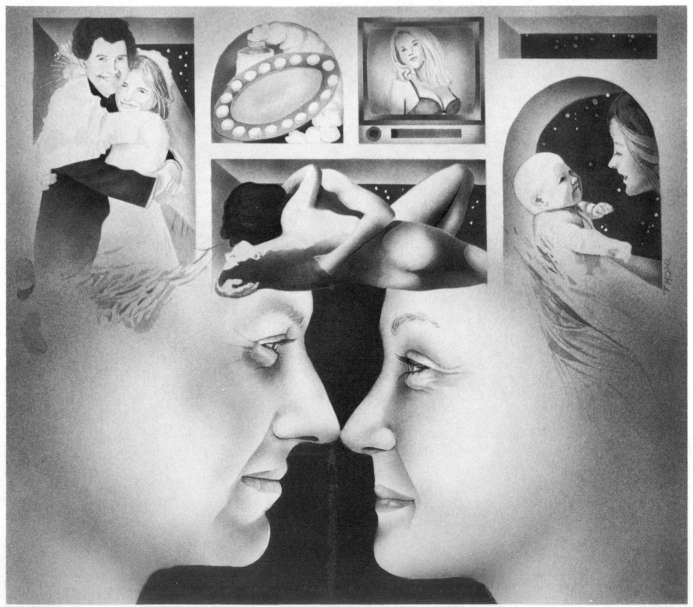

Plate 2
(left) Artist: Wilson McLean. Title: "The Naked Soldier"   Media: Acrylics on canvas.

Plate 3
(top) Artist: Bill Chambers. Art Director: Bill Chambers. Media: Acrylic paints.

Plate 4
(above left) Artist: Fred Otnes. Title: "Paul Revere"   Client: New American Library. Media: Collage and mixed media on linen.

Plate 5
(above right) Artist: John Collier. Client: CBS Records. Media: Pastels on paper.

Plate 6
(above) Artist: Richard Leech. Client: Yamaha.
Media: Airbrushed watercolors.

Plate 7
(left) Artist: Robert Grossman. Client: New West.
Media: Airbrush.

Opposite page

Plate 8
(above) Artist: Julian Allen. Title: "Atlantic City"
Client: *Weekend* magazine. Media: Watercolors.

Plate 9
(bottom left) Artist: Marta Thoma. Client: Boom/
Graphics for Foot Gear. Art Director: Gary
Nichamin. Media: Watercolors and colored inks.

Plate 10
(below right) Artist: Marta Thoma. Media:
Colored inks similar to artwork for *Playboy*.

Plate 11
(left) Artist: Paul Pratchenko. Title: "Newspaper" Client: Boise Cascade Corporation; Dancer, Fitzgerald, Sample San Francisco Agency. Art Director: Kirk Henshaw. Media: Acrylics on canvas. Copyright © Boise Cascade Corporation.

Plate 12
(below left) Artist: Marta Thoma. Client: Boom/ Graphics for Foot Gear. Art Director: Gary Nichamin. Media: Watercolors, colored inks, and acrylics.

Plate 13
(below right) Artist: Brad Holland.

Opposite page

Plate 14
Artist: Bruce Wolfe. Client: Levi Strauss & Co.— Youthwear Division. Art Director: Chris Blum. Media: Casein underpainting with oils. Copyright © Levi Strauss & Co.

Plate 15
(left) Artist: Bernie Fuchs. Title: "Words by Heart"
Client: Reader's Digest Condensed Books. Media:
Oil paints.

Plate 16
(below) A range of color values from dark to light.

Plate 17
(bottom) Color wheel.

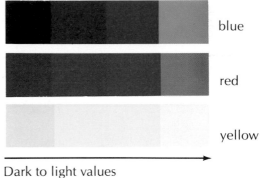

blue

red

yellow

→ Dark to light values

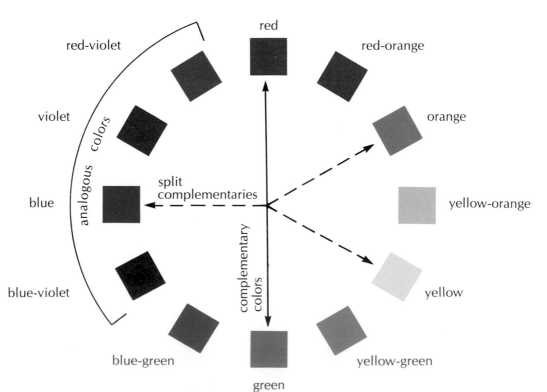

red

red-violet   red-orange

violet   orange

analogous colors

blue   split complementaries   yellow-orange

blue-violet   yellow

complementary colors

blue-green   yellow-green

green

Paint or Ink. Dilute to the consistency of thin ink. If you are going to spray several colors, it is worthwhile to have each color diluted and ready ahead of time. Your set-up may consist of 10 paper cups in a row, each containing a different color paint mixed for a particular part of the painting and diluted to the right consistency, all ready for use. Of course, you can always make adjustments as you go—by adding more red to the purple or thinning the yellow and so on—but thorough preparation permits you to focus your creative attention on the actual spraying after you begin.

X-acto Knife and Scissors. The X-acto knife can be used to pick up and replace the frisket stencils as you spray. (This process is fully explained later.) The scissors are handy for cutting movable stencils and other odd jobs.

Painter's Mask. In the process of airbrushing, small particles are released into the air, and they do not settle immediately. Since it is not healthy to inhale these particles, you will want to purchase a comfortable mask to wear for your own protection. Paper disposable masks, sold in paint and hardware stores for house painters, are good if they can be adjusted to fit snugly against the bridge of your nose. More sophisticated masks are even more protective and block out vapor as well as paint particles. Open a window or door for good ventilation, and take frequent breaks from your work to step outside and breathe fresh air. Wearing a mask for a long period of time is uncomfortable, but do not airbrush

68 Artwork partially airbrushed.

69 Wearing a paper mask while airbrushing keeps you from inhaling large particles of paint. More protective styles of masks are recommended for extensive use of the airbrush.

68

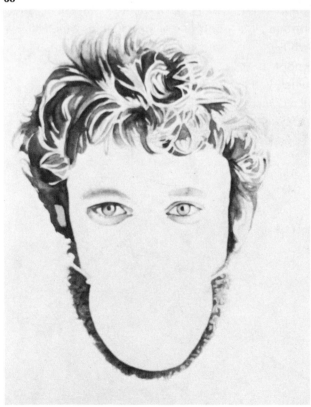

69

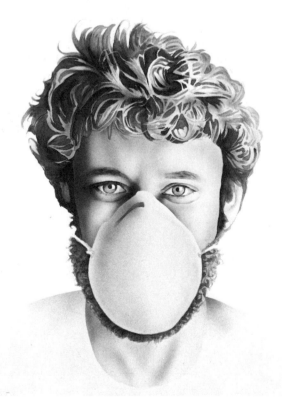

without one! Airbrushing will be more enjoyable if you take these small precautions.

Illustration Ready to Spray.   This is the good paper or illustration board on which you will airbrush. By the time you are ready to spray, the following preliminary steps have been taken:

1. Transferring the rough (as described in *Chapter one*). When you are finished with this step, the illustration will be sketched in very light pencil lines.

2. Making the spray plan. Ask yourself, "Where do I want crisp edges and separate colors in this illustration?" It is around those areas that you will cut a stencil. For example, in the ice cream cone illustration, the sharply defined forms are the ice cream, the cone, and the checkered texture of the cone. The ice cream texture, on the other hand, is soft and will be painted with the airbrush freehand, with no stencil.

3. Cutting the frisket. Frisket paper is an ideal stencil paper for airbrushing. It is a transparent paper with lightly gummed backing that will not tear at the texture of your paper when you pull it up after spraying, and it comes in sheets or rolls, mounted on waxed paper. Cut a piece of frisket paper

slightly larger than the dimensions of your drawing. Peel off the waxed paper and lay the frisket paper, sticky side down, on the drawing. Using an X-acto knife with a #11 blade, cut along the pencil lines that define the areas you will spray in differing colors and tones. Use a sharp blade and press gently so you do not go through your good paper. With a little practice, you will learn just how much pressure is required. Cut the border lines of the illustration if color is to bleed to the sides of the design.

You may have a simple design with only a few lines to cut or you may spend half a day cutting the stencils for a complex design. Either way, when you are finished you can look forward to the fun part, spraying the artwork.

AIRBRUSH TECHNIQUES

Spraying Distance.   The control button is only one of the variables which affects the character of the spray. Distance from the

70 Ice cream cone in three stages.

71 Airbrushed ice cream cone.

paper is another. This may vary from less than 1 inch to 6 inches. When you spray close to the paper, the paint droplets are concentrated. As you pull the airbrush back, the spray becomes fuller and less concentrated.

Spraying Evenly. Adjust the spray on scrap paper before you start on the artwork. Ask yourself: Is it fine enough? Should it be broader? and so on. Experiment with the control button and the distance from the paper until you are satisfied. When the spray looks right, move it onto the artwork without stopping.

To spray evenly, your hand should be constantly moving on and off the artwork. It is best to spray in "passes" so that you have time after each stroke to plan where to spray next. If you hesitate to think about your movements while you are spraying the artwork, the paint will build up unevenly as your hand stalls.

Spraying Large Areas. Holding the airbrush 6 inches from the paper is ideal for spraying large, even tones, as in a sky. Because the spray is full and less concentrated at this distance, there is less risk of spraying unevenly. Spray from left to right, then right to left, beginning and ending each stroke off the artwork. Keep the airbrush at a uniform distance as you pass over the paper, and watch where you are directing the spray. Several passes over the paper will intensify the color.

Spraying a Tonal Gradation. This is a dark tone that gradually becomes lighter and lighter. Spray this area in passes, as described above, but make more passes over the area you want to be the darkest. If, for example, you are spraying a blue sky that is much lighter than at the horizon, pass over the high point of the sky many

times, the midpoint a few times, and the horizon not at all. If you are spraying from 6 inches away, a very light tone will fall on the horizon during the other passes.

Color Blends. Spraying passes of one color next to passes of another color will blend them together softly to make a third color. This is a simple blending technique. As you become more experienced with the airbrush, you will discover many pleasing ways to blend colors.

Detailed Airbrushing. Many images will require detailed airbrushing, without the use of stencils to define them. This is true of soft images, such as the contours on a face, clouds in a sky, or the ripples of the ice cream in the ice cream cone illustration in this chapter.

While working with small details, it is helpful to have an airbrush which will produce a very fine spray. For the smallest details, the brush can be held very close to the paper, close enough to make a soft, fine line.

Make several short passes when you are doing detailed work. Start the airbrush on a small piece of scrap paper if you are working on an interior detail. Hold the paper an inch or more off the artwork with your free hand so that you do not catch the silhouette of the scrap paper when you begin to spray. To end the pass in an interior situation, lift the airbrush straight up very quickly to avoid making a blob.

Movable Stencils. This is simply a cut-out design that you spray over repeatedly, holding it down with your fingers and changing its position each time. The paper stencil should be thick enough to take a soaking from several

72 Artist: Doug Johnson
Client: Schenley Imports
Art Director: Gerry Diebart
Media: Airbrush and drawing media

Doug Johnson is a master of both realistic and interpretive product illustration. In this advertisement for Scotch whiskey, the product appears in an insert designed unobtrusively as part of the total composition, looking not only realistic but superrealistic. Johnson exaggerates the shine of the whiskey bottle with multiple reflections and numerous highlights. The result is a shiny, delectable-looking product. The man and the landscape used to complete the design are treated in a similar superrealistic technique.

At the outset, Johnson makes what he describes as a very rough layout, using blobs of paint to determine the general composition and color of the illustration. After he is satisfied with the design, he uses photo references to improve and define the idea. Then he makes a tightly rendered pencil drawing for the client's approval.

For the finished art, he uses a combination of airbrush and freehand painting. He paints on kid-finish illustration board, working at least twice the reproduction size. To transfer the rough drawing onto the illustration board, he draws the design in reverse on vellum and rubs it, graphite side down, on the board. He uses frisket paper to mask area for airbrushing, cutting the frisket with a swivel knife. With transparent watercolors in the airbrush, he sprays an underpainting on the entire composition. Later, he paints on top of the airbrushed art with gouache. The watercolors are sometimes mixed with a fixative so that they do not bleed when the gouache is painted over them. Johnson also touches up the images with colored pencils.

sprays. If puddles form, dab them off and let the paper dry before you spray again. This is a fast and fun way to make textures or interesting patterns.

Spraying Over Textures. You can experiment with the airbrush by discovering different textures to spray through. Lace, mesh, and cheesecloth make wonderful textures and effective illustrations if you use them selectively. I have used lace for a wallpaper effect in an illustration which pictured a room with a woman gazing into an ornate mirror. I judged that a lace pattern in the background would be companionable, stenciled everything but the wallpaper with frisket paper, and laid the lace on the paper. I then fastened it securely because I wanted a sharp image. After several passes over the lace, I had an interesting looking wallpaper pattern.

There are many original textures waiting to be discovered. Go through the garage, the sewing basket, or "junk" drawers for likely candidates.

Airbrushing with Frisket Paper.   When you have finished cutting a frisket stencil on your artwork as described earlier, you are ready to spray the artwork. Remove a piece of frisket paper with the help of an X-acto knife, as you would take a piece out of a puzzle. Spray the area that is now uncovered. Save the piece of frisket so that you can replace it when you are ready to spray another "part of the puzzle." Let the freshly painted area dry before a frisket is laid back on top of it. One by one, spray all of the parts of the puzzle. Save all of the frisket pieces until you are sure you do not need them. Very small pieces may not be able to withstand repeated use and may have to be recut.

Suggested Exercises

1. Draw a line illustration and enclose it in an outline. Make the illustration very simple with just a few lines to divide the picture into a maximum of five puzzle-like pieces. Apply a frisket on top and cut the lines of the illustration. Remove one piece of frisket at a time, airbrush the exposed area, then replace the frisket. Do the above exercise with (1) black ink, slightly diluted, and (2) colored inks.

2. Draw a more complex line illustration to airbrush, and try these techniques in the illustration:
   • A texture to spray through on one part of the illustration
   • Liquid frisket for small details

3. Make an illustration that combines the techniques of airbrushing with freehand painting using watercolors or acrylics.

Color Separations

Most color artwork today is prepared for printing in a photographer's workshop. By photographing the artwork through filters, the photographer produces a separate negative for each of the four basic colors: red, yellow, blue, and black. In many modern shops, the negative-making process is assisted by a computer to improve the accuracy of the color registration and the color intensity. The illustrator is usually not involved in this technical process except to check to see if the artwork is true in color when it is finally printed. If the photographer and printer are good technicians, the reproduction should have the texture and colors of the original artwork.

TWO-COLOR SEPARATION

The cost of printing four colors is nearly four times the cost of printing black and white, or any other single color. To compromise on cost, some textbooks and other publications are printed in two colors. Black ink or another dark color is usually used for the type, and the second color may be added to charts and illustrations to jazz up what would otherwise be colorless pages.

Unlike most full-color reproduction, the color separation for two-color artwork is usually prepared by the illustrator. The artist makes two drawings, one for each color, so that they are in perfect register with one another. Accurate register is imperative to prevent the color from bleeding into areas it should not cover or from shrinking away from its border leaving a white line. You have probably seen a drawing printed out of register like this. It looks as if someone could not "color within the lines" or makes you feel like you are seeing double.

To register two drawings together, the artist prepares one as an overlay of the other. This technique also applies to three- and four-color hand-separated art, which may require two or three overlays.

What exactly is an overlay? It is a sheet of paper or acetate that is mounted on top of the first drawing with tape along the top side. The tape holds the overlay securely, although it can be lifted up like a flap when the printer photographs the artwork. An overlay is made of paper or plastic transparent enough to see through. A light table helps by increasing the transparency when you make the drawing for the second color on the overlay. The two colors should always be drawn to overlap very slightly. If the original is a line drawing, the lines of the color overlay should meet the *outer edge* of the lines on the original to ensure that the second color will print on top of the line, but not beyond it.

To preserve the register if the tape slips, plastic stick-on register symbols are applied on three or four corners of the original illustration, outside the picture area. On each subsequent overlay, register marks are placed directly over the ones below, to match the "cross." The "cross" should appear to be one, even if there are several overlays. If they look double, lift the faulty overlay and reapply the register marks correctly. Accurate register marks

enable the printer to align the artwork perfectly despite any shift or slackening of the tape.

Neither overlay for a two-color illustration is actually made in color. All of the artwork is completed in a black-and-white medium—whether it will be printed in green, dark brown, pink—because black works well photographically. Sometimes red is substituted for black. When ruby-red film is used, it acts photographically like black and can later be printed in another color.

A simple way to make a two-color illustration is to use black and white and "color" in areas with the second color. The second color, in this case, is not actually drawn; it is indicated for the printer with a cut stencil or a line drawing. Either method is faster than making a second drawing. These two shortcuts are called the "coloring book methods," and they are described below.

Coloring Book Method #1.   In this method, the important parts of the design for the illustration are completed in one of the black-on-white techniques— pen-and-ink, watercolor wash, and so on. As you make the black-on-white drawing, consider where you would like to add areas of flat color to bring another tone to the drawing. Take this into acocunt, and leave areas with less tone, assuming you will add color there later.

The second color may overlap the first to make a third. If the first color is black, the gray tones in shaded areas will subdue the second color. Use a color guide from the printer or the paint store to see what the third color will look like. There are many shades of blue, red, and other colors that look different when they print on top of gray or another color.

Once you have decided where you would like the second color, you must decide what intensity you want in each area. Upon request, your client or the printer can provide you with a color guide that shows the second color printed through varying densities of screened photographic film. The screening will range from 15 percent, which prints the ink very lightly, to 100 percent, which prints the ink at its full intensity. A red ink printed through a 15-percent screen will look pale pink; at 40 percent it will look pink; and at 100 percent it will look nearly red. Using these percentiles in 5-percent increments from 15 to 100 percent, decide what intensity you would like in each area and make notes to yourself.

Use ruby-red film, an acetate with a red film adhering to it, to make the guide for the second color. Red film is good for this application because it is transparent enough but functions photographically as black. It is available in art or graphic supply stores. You will also need an X-acto knife to cut the film.

The black-on-white art must be either mounted or drawn on illustration board so that there is a firm support for the ruby-red film overlay. Cut a piece of the film slightly larger than the illustration but smaller than the board. Place the film on top of the transparent overlay acetate side down, film side up, and tape it securely along the top edge.

Cut along the edges of the areas where you want the second color to be printed, using a sharp X-acto knife. Take care to cut only the red film, not the acetate. Peel away the film over the areas where the second color will not be used.

On another piece of paper make a rough sketch of the design made by the ruby-red overlay. Indicate on this paper the percentage of the color screen intended on each part. This will serve as a guide for the printer to follow.

Add the register marks to the black-and-white illustration underneath and match them with those on the ruby-red film overlay.

There are two useful color guides available to the artist. The PMS booklet of ink colors and their composition is used by all printers. Every ink color is pictured and numbered, so that colors are standardized for all printers, making it a handy reference for illustrators choosing colors for their drawings. The book is available at printing shops and art stores.

The *Communication Arts Color Guide for Offset Lithography* is especially helpful when you are choosing two or three colors for an illustration because it not only displays samples of all the different inks but also shows the colors produced when they are mixed with second and third colors. In the book, each color is broken down into various screen percentages and shown in combination with screens of other colors. With this device you can see what unique color will result from blending the inks in various proportions or from using screens of varying densities. The book also explains some color printing tricks, such as printing red to enrich the black, and it can be used to help you decide what screen percentages to select for the artwork.

The *Communication Arts Color Guide* is available in coated and uncoated paper stock. The colors printed on coated stock are more brilliant because uncoated paper tends to absorb the color more, dulling its brilliance. However, the less expensive uncoated stock edition may be the more

73

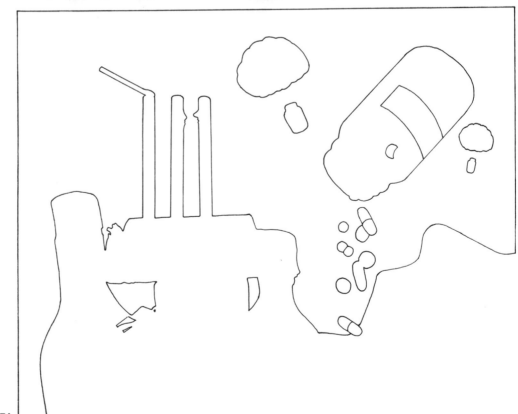

74

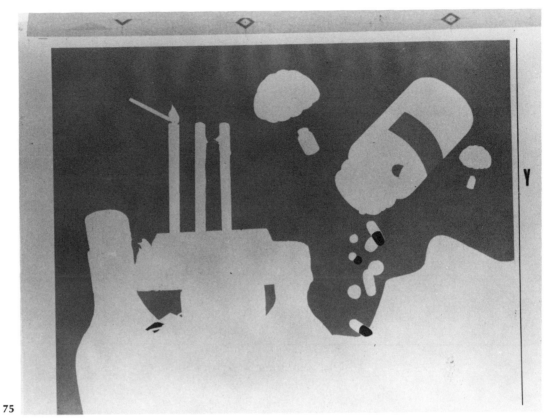

75

73 Artist: Marta Thoma
Client: Benjamin/Cummings Publishing Company

74 Color separation line work.

75 Color separation tone.

practical choice for you. It is often used for color decisions involved in two- or three-color artwork.

Coloring Book Method #2. This is another method of adding flat areas of color to an otherwise-finished black-and-white illustration. It is identical to the previous method except that instead of cutting stencils to indicate where the second color belongs, the artist simply outlines the areas with pen and ink on a tracing paper overlay. Printers with modern equipment can use the guidelines to photographically cover those outlined areas with a tone of flat color. Consult

with your client and the printer for the job before you use this method, to be sure if they can work with the guidelines.

If you are given the go-ahead by the printer, make a black-and-white drawing which defines the major design and details of the illustration. Then outline on the tracing paper overlay the sections which will print in the second color.

Draw the guidelines with a fine line, like the one made by a #0 ink pen tip. For the method to work, the guidelines must enclose an area completely, leaving no gaps. Follow the lines of the original precisely.

Again you must choose what kind of screen you want for each colored area. Should it be orange, light orange, or pale orange? Use a sky-blue colored pencil to make notes on the overlay, since this color does not show up photographically. In the margin of the overlay indicate the percentage, for example, "50 percent screened orange," and draw a light blue pencil line to the area indicated. Make a separate notation for each area outlined on the overlay. Apply three register marks to the black-and-white drawing and to the tracing paper overlay.

Integrated Two-Color Illustration. This method is used when the second color plays a relatively important part in the design of the illustration. The drawing for the second color may be as involved and detailed as the first-color drawing; both are done in a black-and-white medium. While it is aesthetically more pleasing than the "coloring book" methods just discussed, this approach is also more difficult and time-consuming.

The second-color drawing is made on an overlay so that it will be in perfect register with the first color. You can choose from several mediums to make the second color, but keep in mind that they must be used on a transparent surface that will function as an overlay. The following is a guide to suggested overlay materials for various art mediums:

Medium: pen and ink
Overlay: vellum

Medium: line work, crosshatching, or the like
Overlay: tracing paper, clear acetate, or frosted acetate

Medium: watercolor wash, ink wash, pencils, crayons, or airbrush
Overlay: frosted acetate

Surfaces such as illustration board and most drawing paper are obviously impractical. Frosted acetate is excellent

because, although it is transparent, it has a paper-like texture which works well with watercolors as well as with inks and pencils.

When choosing the images to render in the second color, decide on the basis of what is appropriate to the subject. Let us say, for example, you are working with dark brown and green as your two colors. If the illustration has a human face, you would not want to render it on an overlay marked for green, unless you intend to create a sickly or surreal effect. In general, warm colors like browns, oranges, or reds are natural for faces and skin tones. Greens, blues, and purples are best in landscapes and nature scenes. Any color can be used on inanimate objects like clothing, furniture, and houses.

If the second color is done in a medium other than line drawing or crosshatching, it will be photographed through a halftone screen to pick up the fine tone. The photographer shoots the artwork through a rectangular window the size of the illustration. A pattern of small dots will be printed within this window area. Even white areas will have a shadow of dot patterns. This can pose problems in some illustrations because the dots may be desirable in some parts of the design but not in others. There may be times when the artist does not want even a hint of color in the white areas—as in the case of a silhouette, where any color outside the silhouette blurs the effect. In any circumstance where the artist wants to confine the color, he or she must make a custom-made "window" through which the photographer can shoot the artwork.

The custom-made silhouette window is made as an overlay, either with stencils of ruby-red film, as described in Coloring

Book Method #1, or as the pen-and-ink outline on tracing paper described in Coloring Book Method #2. In either case, add register marks as always to an overlay.

THREE- & FOUR-COLOR SEPARATION

More than a decade ago, it was customary for illustrators to prepare the artwork for three- and four-color separations. This technique was commonly used in elementary textbooks and in other children's books. It was sometimes called "fake color" for reasons that are not entirely clear. Today, more textbooks and children's books are made with photographic four-color separations, but for those occasions when hand-cut three- and four-color separations are still required, it is worth discussing the techniques.

Basically, three- and four-color illustrations are prepared in the same way as two-color art, except that additional overlays are required for each new color. Any of the methods discussed for making a second-color overlay can be used for a third and fourth color. All of the overlays must be carefully registered on each other.

Each additional overlay adds to the number of possible color combinations. A two-color illustration contains the potential for three combinations, as well as many variations in the light and dark values created by screened percentages. With the addition of a third color, the possible color combinations more than triple, and just about any hue can be made with four colors. It is, therefore, necessary to have a color chart on hand to plan the intricate color combinations in your drawing.

PHOTOGRAPHIC FOUR-COLOR SEPARATION

For a four-color separation, the artwork is photographed four times through different colored filters to make transparencies of all four necessary colors, the primaries—yellow, magenta, cyan (dark blue)—and black. The red filter produces the cyan transparency; the green filter, the magenta transparency; and the blue filter, the yellow transparency.

When combined and printed, yellow, magenta, and cyan should be able to reproduce all the colors in the original artwork. However, impurities in the printing ink often necessitate color corrections in the transparencies so that the image does not appear muddy. Another problem is the lack of density in shadow areas. This is solved by improving the contrast in the picture with the addition of black. A black transparency is made by photographing the artwork through a yellow filter or through a combination of all three primary filters.

The artwork is photographed through a screen so that each transparency is made up of thousands of tiny dots. The colors you see in printed artwork are produced by the optical mixing of the four colors of dots.

The quality of paper used will affect the quality of the color reproduction. A bright, smooth, white paper will reproduce colors best. The rougher the paper, the duller and more distorted the colors will be.

To make a four-color separation, it is necessary to learn how to use a copy camera. Printing and photographic skills of this nature are taught in books and classes on graphic art production.

Taking Care of Your Finished Illustration

When you have finished a drawing or painting for an illustration, the artwork should be treated properly. Unless it has been done on illustration board or canvas, the artwork should be mounted on board to keep it from bending or wrinkling and to provide a support for handling. A tissue overlay is placed over the art to protect it from fingerprints and other surface damage and mounted so that it can be easily flipped aside to view and photograph the artwork.

Illustrations are never matted as framed art is. The mat would cover the area meant for bleed. Even if the edges of your drawing look rough or uneven, resist the urge to cover them with a mat. If you have allowed for bleed in the illustration by increasing the dimensions ½ inch on all four sides, the uneven edges of your drawing will be neatly trimmed in the photographic or trimming processes.

ARTWORK ON PAPER

Drawings or paintings on paper should be mounted on white illustration or mat board. If the art paper has a border, it should be trimmed so that it is even, about 1 to 2 inches on all sides. The paper is placed in the center of the white board to create equal space top and bottom and side to side. Secure the paper to the board with tape, preferably a white cloth tape, which will not tear the paper if it has to be removed or adjusted. The tape is usually used in two long strips top and bottom or as four shorter strips centered on the sides of the art. It should look neat and even.

A piece of tissue paper, tracing paper, or plastic acetate can be used for a protective overlay, which should be cut to cover the whole of the art paper but should not extend beyond the board. This should be secured with one long strip of tape along the top of the white board.

If the artwork already has one or more overlays mounted on top of it, a protective overlay should cover the top one and be mounted on the outer edge of the board so that it does not interfere with the other overlays.

ARTWORK ON ILLUSTRATION BOARD

Artwork on illustration board should be planned so that there is at least a 2- to 4-inch border of white around the image area. Cloth masking tape can be used to make a clean edge on a finished painting, or the image area can be defined with a light pencil line. A border area is necessary so that the board can be handled without touching the artwork. It also provides a surface for mounting a protective overlay.

A tissue or tracing paper overlay is mounted on the board and secured with tape along the top edge in the same way described above.

ARTWORK ON CANVAS

Like board, canvas is a sturdy material that will protect the artwork. An oil painting can be sprayed with non-glossy varnish for extra protection once it has thoroughly dried. The problem is that there is rarely enough time left in a schedule for both paint and varnish to dry. Varnish must be left untouched for 48 hours to dry thoroughly.

When canvas is being transported, it should be wrapped in paper for protection. Canvas to be mailed must be packaged in a sturdy wooden crate.

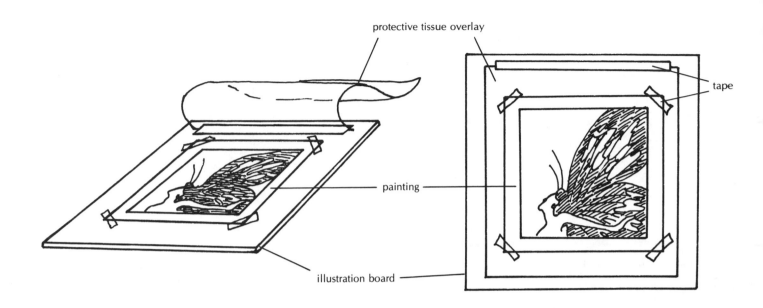

protective tissue overlay

tape

painting

illustration board

76 Taking care of an illustration.

77 Artist: Fred Otnes
Client: Time-Life
Media: Collage and mixed media
Otnes creates a different world by rearranging photo
images and developing them with his varied techniques. The composition and arrangement of each
image are carefully planned. He sometimes uses a
landscape or, in this case, a baseball stadium to contain and unify the images.

Chapter
four
Communicating
Your Idea

To improve communicating skills, we will examine what goes on in an illustration to make someone else understand it. Since symbols are the key to communication, we will explore the different kinds of symbols and how they should work to communicate your idea. In this chapter, we will not find the formula for the perfect illustration, but we will discover how to adjust and improve an illustration in process.

An illustration develops continually, from the first idea you visualize in your mind to drawing that idea on paper. In *Chapter one* we describe the process of making exploratory thumbnail sketches and then firming the idea up in a rough drawing. At each stage, you must make more decisions about what the imagery will look like and how it will be arranged on the page. When the illustration is completed, you will inevitably ask yourself two questions about the success of the artwork: "Does it look the way I wanted it to?" and "Do other people immediately understand and appreciate the message?" If your answer to both questions is "maybe" or "no," somewhere along the line you should have made some different decisions.

78 Artist: Marta Thoma
Media: colored inks

If your answer to both questions is always "yes," you are very lucky. It is fair to say that at one time or another nearly every artist is unhappy with the way a particular idea has been executed. The point of this chapter is to learn a method of analyzing symbolic content in a drawing so that when something "isn't right," you can understand why and learn how to improve it or make a better drawing next time.

An illustration is made up of symbols on many different levels. If you can learn to recognize the symbols and what they are communicating, you can learn how to improve your artwork. You must know what parts are communicating well and what parts are not helping. Once this is clear, you should be able to adjust your work to express your ideas more successfully.

Cultural Images & Content Symbols

Cultural images express ideas that relate to the way of life of a given people at a given time, as in our Western culture, for example. Since we share many similar life experiences with each other, we react in a similar way to pictorial images that remind us of those experiences.

We grow up in some kind of family or other. We go to elementary school and read similar books there. We learn science, math, and reading, go out for recess, and learn games. We learn to play the popular sports in our culture such as football and baseball, jump rope, marbles, and jacks. Similar experiences go on endlessly throughout school and into the world of work. Television, radio, and newspapers keep us up-to-date about fashions, humor, and political events in our culture.

From this vast, similar experience, we can draw endless pictorial imagery filled with symbolism about our culture. To be good at recognizing this kind of symbol, you must be alert to what is going on in the world around you.

Here are some examples of images and

what they generally symbolize:

- Heart—love or romance. A broken heart symbolizes a lost love or a painful end to romance. The heart image has been especially popularized by Valentine's Day. Exchanging valentines in elementary school taught us what a red heart meant.

- New Porsche—wealth, since it is an expensive automobile. It also symbolizes modern technology and potential speed.

- Woman in a business suit carrying a briefcase—a successful businesswoman. It has connotations of "women's liberation."

- Church—Christianity and religion. It may also symbolize comfort, morality, tyranny, or a wedding, depending on the other information in the drawing.

- Blood—pain, death, violence, aggression, war. This is a universal symbol.

- Mountain lion—nature, a wild creature, danger.

- Cat curled up sleeping—contentment, comfort, and maybe an easy life.

- Monkey in a tuxedo—humor. A joke is being made by comparing a monkey to

79

people since it is wearing human clothing.

None of the above descriptions are specific, so they should be considered general symbols only. The details of their symbolic content will be filled in later when we take into consideration gestures, attitudes, relationships between images, and composition. In other words, we do not know the full story about these images. Is the Porsche in a parking lot or about to be driven off a cliff? Is the church a seedy building in the slums or a great cathedral? There is much to consider.

The Relationship of Images

Another level of symbolic communication is created by the relationship of one image to another. Something completely different can be implied about an image if it is placed in different contexts. For example, compare these two pictures, which contain an identical mountain lion.

1. A mountain lion creeping along a rock in a wild environment.

2. A mountain lion creeping along a sidewalk in a suburban neighborhood.

The first picture is a natural scene which describes the mountain lion and the places where it is expected to be found. The main point of interest is the animal itself. Its creeping position may make you wonder if it is going to pounce on some prey it is stalking.

The second picture is an unnatural scene that brings up several questions. Has the mountain lion escaped from the zoo? Are the people in the neighborhood in danger? If there are people in the picture, you will probably know the answer to that question; if they look frightened, you can guess that it is a dangerous situation, but if a boy is strolling along beside the mountain lion with a big grin on his face, the picture is supposed to be humorous and not frightening. In any case, the situation is the main point of interest instead of the mountain lion itself.

Every image in a picture relates to every other image to tell the full story. If your illustration images are going to tell the story so that it communicates your idea effectively, the images must enhance each other. Ask yourself these questions about the relationship of images:

• Are the relationships clear enough? For example, if one person is shaking hands with another, it should be clear that they are not wrestling.
• Is the main subject clear? Other images should not upstage the important information in an illustration. Every image should advance the main idea.

In fantasy or surreal illustrations, images relate to each other in a more complicated manner. The fantasy or surreal quality is actually created by the unusual relationships between one image and another. This is not to say that offbeat relationships are chosen in a haphazard or

79 Artist: Robert Steiner
Title: *Detail of Expulsion*

80 Artist: Marta Thoma
Client: *San Francisco Magazine*
Media: Black watercolor wash

arbitrary way in an attempt to be weird. On the contrary, these images and their interrelationships must be selected very carefully to make the subject of the illustration clear. In a successful piece of work of this type, the subject is very obvious, although it has been expressed in a kind of poetry of images.

The distortions and strange relationships in a fantasy illustration call attention to themselves, and because they stand out, they must be gauged by the symbolic impact created. For example, drawing a person on a much smaller scale than the environment creates the symbolic feeling of powerlessness. If a story you are illustrating is about a businessman who feels inadequate and unable to do his job, it may be an appropriate distortion to draw the man looking much smaller than his desk and office.

Some of the common kinds of distortion made in fantasy or surreal illustrations include:

1. Distorting the size relationship of images.
2. Changing the property of objects (a rubber-like pencil, a house that floats in the air).
3. Exchanging attributes of one object and another (a tree-like person, a panther-like car, a castle-like house).
4. Changing the context in which a subject is ordinarily found (an elephant in a tree, an airplane in a swimming pool, a ballet dancer on a roof).
5. Exaggerating features (an enormous tongue or feet, tiny head).

When you are planning a fantasy or surreal illustration, you still must answer certain questions. Are the relationships clear enough? Are the distortions appropriate to the subject matter? Does the main subject stand out?

Gestures & Attitudes of Images

Much can be told about people by looking at their facial expressions and how they are standing, moving, and gesturing with their hands. A drawing of a person also has all of this information. The way the hands are drawn will tell whether the person is tense, excited, self-conscious, or relaxed. The figure may be active or look frozen and emotionless, like a doll. How the figure is positioned in a picture is important—whether it is turned away, which may mean secrecy, mystery, or despair, or confronting the viewer actively in a frontal position. If the eyes are looking away from the viewer, the mood is more passive and uneasy than if the eyes stare out at the viewer in active confrontation. Facial expressions, of course, can convey a wide range of emotions—fear, anger, grief, joy, laughter, determination, frustration, pride, exhaustion, happiness, and so on.

It is fairly obvious to talk about the ways face or posture evoke particular emotions. But do you think about the emotions communicated by the nonhuman images in an illustration—the plants, refrigerators, or clouds? Every image, from an inanimate object to the background scenery, has its own gesture and attitude, and these images can communicate emotions as powerfully as the human figure can.

You have probably heard someone describe a house as looking "tired" or "sad," or a car as "sexy." Human emotions or qualities are often ascribed to objects. When we use words like sad, happy, mean, gentle, or loving to describe things rather than people, we are, in point of fact, describing a human feeling. These words tell others how *we* feel when *we* look at the object: a droopy, unkempt house evokes a feeling of tiredness in us, so we attribute the fatigue to the house.

The gesture and attitude of an image help to determine what kind of human emotion it communicates. If a tree, for example, looks strong and full, it will evoke emotions of strength and happiness. If it droops with sparse limbs, it will evoke sadness.

Every image in an illustration should work toward communicating the overall idea or feeling, and the gesture and attitude of each should personify the human emotion appropriate to the mood of the piece. For example, let us say you are illustrating a mystery short story. After reading the story, you decide that the prevailing mood of your illustration will be terror. You have decided that the drawing will include a close-up of a terrified woman's face, the hall behind her, and a grandfather clock described in the story. The mood of the hall and grandfather clock should reflect the fear in the woman's face. The hall should look dark and dangerous. The clock could look mean and evil, as if it were causing the woman's fear, or terrified itself, reflecting the fear in the woman's face. Of course, there will be details in the story to help you decide which emotion is appropriate. The point is that every image, according to how you draw it and the qualities you draw into it, will have its own part in the story and will add to the mood of the illustration.

Images can successfully add to the mood of an illustration in two ways. The first is for all of the images to reflect the same emotion—in the mystery illustration, the woman, the hall, and the clock all look frightened. When every image reinforces one emotion, it becomes a powerful message. The second way is for images to personify different emotions and create a kind of conversation with one another, just as a group of figures can appear to be having a conversation. This is what would happen if the woman in the mystery illustration looked frightened, and the hall and clock looked mean and threatening. The tension created between the woman and the other elements would intensify the mood. Picture a room with three figures. One figure is pointing a gun at a woman who is screaming, while a dark figure stands watching. The figure with the gun can be compared to a threatening-looking grandfather clock, while the dark mysterious figure is like the dark hall.

A conflicting mood between one image and another will stand out like a sore thumb if it is a mistake. Take, for example, the same story illustration. If you draw the hall to look bright and cheerful with smiling portraits on the walls, it will create quite a contrast next to a threatening-looking clock and a frightened woman's face. If this odd contrast is part of the story being told, the drawing would be appropriate. If there is no mention of a friendly hall in the story, the illustration will be confusing and will project conflicting moods and an unclear message.

How do you draw an image that looks

Woody Allen

81 Artist: Edward Sorel
Title: *Woody Allen*
Client: *Village Voice*
Media: Pen-and-ink

terrified or threatening or sad or elated or in love? Admittedly, this is not always easy to do. The best way to attack the problem is to examine the emotion and decide what kind of physical characteristics would be exhibited by a person feeling this emotion. For example:

Happy: relaxed, robust, smiling with upturned mouth, color in face, good posture, active

Mean and threatening: dark shadows on the face, scowling with a wrinkled brow, pale face, downturned mouth, teeth showing, unhealthy, tense posture and gestures, sharp fingernails, advancing posture as if moving toward a victim

Sad: downturned mouth and eyes, tears, pale face, drooping posture, lack of emotion, unkempt appearance

Excited: bright face, alert eyes, color in cheeks, highly active, gesturing

Determined: attention directed at one point, focused eyes, face, posture, and gesture

Sexy: seductive posture, emphasizing curves, color in face and lips

Now let us apply each of these descriptions to an inanimate object. How would you go about drawing a happy tree, a threatening clock, a sad hat, an excited city, a determined boat, or a sexy car? To draw these, you must translate human expressions of these characteristics to the nonhuman subject and apply the physical characteristics for each emotional attitude to the inanimate subject.

Happy tree: strong, sturdy trunk, full leaves, colorful blossoms

Threatening grandfather clock: sharp corners, metal details, pointed hands, thin and old, gesturing forward, deep shadows, dark colors

Sad hat: drooping, out of shape, wrinkled, and downturned

Excited city: bustling activity, bright lights and colors

Determined boat: actively moving in one direction, moving against a storm or large waves

Sexy car: attractive angles and curves on car, new and shiny, attractive color

AVOIDING AMBIGUOUS MESSAGES

So far we have examined the importance of your choice of image and emotional values. How the image is drawn and where it is placed on the page also affect the communication in a powerful way, but at this juncture we should consider the fact that the power of an image can cause disaster in your illustration.

Try to avoid using imagery that is too personal, the kind that no one but you will understand. Images should be chosen directly from the illustration assignment, and they should communicate a general idea clearly. If visual imagery can be compared to the spoken language, this is like warning you not to give a speech in pig Latin. Even if you and a circle of friends speak it to each other, you can bet that not many people in a large audience will understand the message if you speak in pig Latin.

Here is an example of this kind of mistake, taken from a classroom experience. The class had been given an assignment to illustrate an article on hypnotism. One student produced a rough drawing dominated by the image of a large rabbit. Since there was no mention of a rabbit in the article, he was asked why he chose this image. The student said, "I always think of rabbits when I think of hypnotism because of their beady eyes." Rabbits symbolized hypnotism to *this* student. The problem was that rabbits do not, generally, symbolize hypnotism and no one else would have understood the illustration.

The connection between rabbits and hypnotism was the student's personal imagery. Most of us have symbolic attachments to certain images. If your grandfather always gave you candy when you were a child, you may grow up to think about grandfathers or elderly gentlemen whenever you see candy. Candy will have taken on a personal symbolism for you. However, if you use this personal symbolism in an illustration and depend on it to communicate a message about grandfathers, no one will understand. A box of candy will not symbolize "grandfather" to anyone else.

Many personal images are cultural images as well, and so they can be used successfully. For example, if you grew up with a favorite teddy bear which meant comfort to you, teddy bears may still make you think of childhood and comfort. Since many babies are given teddy bears, many adults grow up with similar memories about them. The teddy bear, therefore, is both a personal and a cultural symbol for you.

In summary, it is a good idea to use imagery everyone will understand. However, clichés should be avoided at all costs. Being clear and concise does not exclude originality and interest. It just means that if we don't talk in pig Latin, people can understand our words much better. If the words are clear, they can be used to communicate an infinite number of interesting ideas and, indeed, poetry.

Images whose symbolism is clear have an equal power.

WHAT IS A CLICHÉ?

Since we want to avoid clichéd images, let us define them. A cliché is a saying that has been used over and over to the point of becoming stale—a crime of passion; no use crying over spilled milk. In the art of illustrating, a cliché is an image that has been presented in the same way over and over and has lost its freshness and meaning. The little yellow happy face that became so popular a few years ago is a good example of a cliché image. At first it accompanied the slogan "Have a nice day!" and it was successful at expressing a simple kind of happiness. But before long, the happy face was mass-produced on bumper stickers, t-shirts, hats, stationery, and so on until everyone felt bombarded with the image. It grew so tiresome that some people retaliated by buying bumper stickers that made jokes about the happy face. Obviously, it ceased to convey happiness once it became a cliché image. Because the image was so overused, it came to express commercialism and imbecility.

The happy face is a gross example of a cliché image, but there are many kinds of clichés that are more subtle. For example, a couple holding hands and running on the beach at sunset is an overused representation of romance. And yet, if the same image could be presented in a new way, it could still be enjoyable. The point is to avoid making images exactly like those you have seen. Because clichés may come into your head unconsciously, even when you think you are being original, you must always look at your drawing and ask yourself "Have I seen something just like this many times before?" If the answer is "no," proceed.

Abstract Symbolism

Abstract symbols also work to communicate in an illustration. They are the large and small abstract shapes in the illustration, and they are subtler than the content symbols discussed earlier. Abstract symbols communicate to a viewer on a more subliminal level than content symbols, but communication on this level can have a surprisingly potent effect on the concept and mood in an illustration.

Large abstract symbols are the shapes that make up the general composition of your illustration. The arrangement of the shapes on the page, as well as their color and how thin, thick, dark, or light they are, will affect the mood of the illustration. Large, heavy, dark shapes encircling a small thin shape will be perceived as threatening, while several small lyrical shapes will create a lighthearted mood.

There are no hard, fast rules to tell you what shapes will communicate what specific moods. Most of these decisions must be made intuitively. You can become better at using large abstract symbols and can improve your communication skills simply by being aware of the symbols you are using and questioning yourself. Your intuition will tell you whether they add or detract from the general statement of the illustration. Only when you create a symbol and fail to notice it can it accidentally say something quite different from your intention.

Small, abstract symbols are also important. These are the smallest shapes in your artwork—the brushstrokes, pen marks, or the fine spray of an airbush, which are often determined by the art technique. As the personal hallmark, or "handmark," of the artist, they tell how the artwork was done and what kind of attitude the artist had toward it. For example, a watercolor with obvious brush-strokes expresses casualness toward the work. An even wilder brushstroke expresses abandon and unleashed emotion. In contrast, the smooth controlled spray of paint from an airbrush is less personal but expresses perfection and serenity. Every technique and its

82 Artist: George Stavrinos
Client: Bergdorf/Goodman
Media: Pen-and-ink
This illustration for a Claude Montana design is a serene landscape of geometric shapes that reflect the clothes design. The sharp angles of the jackets' shoulders are reflected in the geometric shape held in front of the figure by a mysterious hand. The dress pattern is complemented by the tile floor and other unexplained spherical shapes.

manner of application makes a different kind of mark that influences the mood of an illustration.

Symbols like these will work best for you if you choose a technique and style to fit the illustration. For example, a personal style is appropriate when warmth or casualness is indicated. Illustrations in children's books often reveal the handmark of the artist undisguised. The cool perfection of an airbrush technique would, in most cases, be inappropriate in a book for young children. Once again, the choice must be based on your intuition, what "feels" right to you.

Communication Checklist

Many different kinds of symbols are present in even the simplest illustration. They should aid in creating the mood and expressing the idea in the work. To be sure that your drawing communicates your idea successfully, ask yourself the following questions:

1. What do the images in your illustration symbolize?
2. Are the symbols cultural, personal, or both?
3. Do the images symbolize the main theme of the illustration assignment?
4. Are the relationships of images in the illustration clear?
5. What is the predominant mood of the illustration?
6. Do the gestures and attitudes of each image in your illustration reflect the mood?
7. Do the abstract symbols in your illustration reflect the mood?
8. Have you chosen an appropriate art technique that enhances the mood?

Suggested Exercises

1. Draw the same image in three different attitudes. For example, draw:
   - A cheerful tree.
   - A threatening tree.
   - A sad tree.

2. Draw three different images, all with the same emotion.
   - Draw a *happy* girl, kite, tree.
   - Draw a *sad* hat, man, hamburger.

3. Draw the following images having a "conversation" with each other:
   - An angry motorcycle, a determined rider, and a trouble-making road.
   - A threatening cloud and a worried house.

4. Review one or more illustrations you have made, answering each of the questions from the preceding Communication Checklist.

Drawing to Communicate

It is more important for an illustrator to learn to draw an easily recognizable subject—to "capture the essence"—than to draw a rendered one. An easily recognizable drawing will have all of the most distinctive characteristics of the subject, which may, at times, be exaggerated for clarity. For example, a puddle of water is recognizable by its shape and its wet look. A wet-looking puddle would be drawn with reflections, since these are characteristic of wetness. A puddle drawn from an angle which affords no reflecting lights or images could be realistic, but not convincing.

Let us consider some subjects—a chair, a glass vase, an apple, a wig, and a mountain—to see what qualities are essential in their descriptions:

Chair: shape
Glass vase: shape and reflection of glass
Apple: shape and color
Wig: shape and texture
Mountain: shape, color, and texture

As you can see, some images are identified primarily by shape, like the chair and the mountain; and other images, like the wig, would be difficult to recognize without texture. Some images are distinguished by color; the apple is most recognizable as red. If the apple is green or yellow, the shape must be very clear to differentiate it from a lemon or a lime. If an apple is orange or purple, it will no longer look like an apple, but will suggest a ball or some other toy.

One of the purposes of drawing characteristic images is to be sure that the image is not confused with something altogether different. Consider a picture of a man with a mountain behind his head. If the mountain is not instantly recognizable as a mountain, it may be mistaken for a hat on top of the man's head.

Decide what qualities are most characteristic of the images you will use before you begin to draw. Remember that these are the features that will communicate the essence of the images. Be sure that you have drawn them correctly before painting or drawing other details. If you are making a simple line drawing, almost every line will be essential to describing the image. If you are making an elaborate painting, the distinguishing characteristics should be considered first before other details and elaborations are added.

Cartoonists are experts at drawing the essential qualities of an image with very little elaboration. A simple object like a chair is drawn so that it is instantly recognizable, even though it is made up of simple lines. If an image is not easily recognizable, the point of the humor or story can be lost.

Drawing Difficult Subjects

It may not be too difficult to capture the essence of an apple with a simple line drawing or color technique. However, some subjects are difficult to capture with either a simple or complex technique. The most difficult ones are those that have little or no color themselves, but reflect the light and color around them, like water, glass, chrome, and other shiny materials. When you draw these subjects, you must include a suggestion of light and reflection in even the simplest drawings.

HOW TO DRAW WATER

If you want to learn to draw water, the first thing to do is dispense with some of the false stereotypes about what water is supposed to look like. In other words,

83 Artist: Bruce Wolfe
Title: *Reaping the Sea*
Client: *Playboy* magazine
Art Director: Art Paul
Media: Casein underpainting with oils
Bruce Wolfe took the title *Reaping the Sea* literally to make this illustration.

water does *not* always look blue and wiggly. Water is found in many places—in the ocean, a pond, or a water pitcher—and it looks different in every form.

Although water itself is colorless, it often reflects the colors and shapes of nearby images. A lake may reflect a blue sky, which makes the water look blue. Light sources like the sun, moon, or artificial light will reflect on water to make bright white highlights.

Not only does water reflect, it can reveal colors from images within it since it is transparent. In a shallow pond, you might see pebbles and the color of the sand on the bottom. Sometimes images are distorted by the water, and they appear larger or misshapen. Consider the various visual effects of water on a rock lying half in and half out of the water at the edge of a pond. The rock will seem to have broken edges at the water line, and the half beneath the water may appear distorted.

Water looks different in motion than it does in a flat calm. A still lake with the sun shining on it will have one major highlight from the reflection of the sun. If you threw a rock into the lake, the water would break into ripples of motion and the single highlight would be broken into multiple highlights, one on each of the ripples. The single highlight could also be broken by a motorboat crossing the lake, creating waves that would each reflect a highlight. Water that is active, like a wave, has a tendency to foam, bubble, and splash. A waterfall, a rainstorm, and water spilling from a drinking fountain are other examples of water in action.

So far, we have discussed the different properties of water and their effects on the appearance of water.

1. Water reflects nearby colors and images. Light sources shining on water reflect as white highlights.
2. Since water is transparent, colors and images below the surface will show through if the water is shallow. Images within the water will appear to be distorted.
3. Water has different properties when it is in motion.

No wonder water is difficult to draw! It has so many characteristics that vary in accordance with how deep it is, whether the sun is shining, what images are nearby, and whether it is flowing or still. One or more of these properties can be present at one time in an image of water, depending on the circumstances. For example, if you are drawing an image of a lake that is still and deep, the water will have primarily a reflecting property, so the scenery near the lake will shimmer on the water like a mirror image. In most cases, however, the water you are drawing will have two or three of the properties listed above simultaneously. For example, if you are drawing a gently moving shallow creek, there may be (1) reflected color from grass, trees, and sky, (2) color and shapes showing through from the bottom, and (3) multiple highlights from the ripples of the moving water. When all of the variables are present, the image of water becomes highly complex.

How do we begin to draw water? Here are some basic categories which break down the appearance of water in various states. Concentrate on one category at a time, using the study technique described below. If you are planning an illustration and have a particular image of water in mind, choose the category that best describes it.

Moving water: (1) shallow; (2) deep; (3) very active, splashing, foaming, and so on

Motionless water: (1) shallow; (2) deep; (3) very shallow puddle, droplets; (4) water in a glass

Find three different photographs of water that fall into the category you have chosen. For example, if you are studying moving water, very active, you will look for three photographs of ocean waves, waterfalls, or something similar. If you are studying motionless water, very shallow, you will look for three photographs of puddles, and so on.

Examine the photographs and copy them. Do the first copy of each in a black-and-white technique like soft pencils. Next, copy the photographs in a color medium like colored pencils or watercolors. If you are not comfortable copying them freehand, use a transfer method (discussed in *Chapter two*) for the important guidelines of the photograph.

Copying the photographs will acquaint you with the basic characteristics of the water in a specific category. The picture you are drawing will probably have several abstract shapes and colors as components of the image. Photographs permit you to examine the image closely to see how the properties of the water create abstract shapes through reflected and revealed images and colors.

After you have made three drawings, study them to see what they have in common. Then make a fourth drawing which combines and simplifies the three earlier drawings. Try to eliminate unimportant details, and include only the shapes that are essential to ensure that the image is "read" as water. The image will probably still have strong reflections and bright highlights when irrelevant details have been left out. If this drawing is successful, you will have "captured the essence" of water.

By making a simplified drawing, you will learn what basic shapes are necessary to make an image look like water. This knowledge is important, even if you intend to paint a detailed illustration, because in a more elaborate version you must accentuate the basic colors and shapes that make the water look wet.

The experience of researching one particular category should prepare you to draw this kind of image for an illustration. Suppose one of the photographs you have copied is a picture of a lake with a mountain and sky reflecting in the water. For an illustration, you would like to draw a lake with an old mill reflecting on the water. Since you have studied and drawn the reflection of a mountain, it should not be too difficult to draw the mill in a similar way, with the same kind of image distortions, muted colors, and other characteristics you noticed.

If you are a beginning artist, it is a good idea to study several of the categories listed earlier in this section. Make three drawings from photographs of each kind of water and make one "shorthand" drawing that condenses the qualities of the three. File these drawings along with the photographs for future reference.

HOW TO DRAW GLASS

Glass has some properties in common with water: it is transparent, and it reflects nearby colors, lights, and images in a similar way. Consequently it, too, presents a complex image.

Glass characteristics vary in accordance with the way it is shaped. Let us divide glass into two categories to study it: (1) flat glass, like windowpanes, and (2) curved glass, like drinking glasses, eyeglasses, and car windshields.

Both flat and curved glass reveal images behind them. The important difference between the two is the way reflections fall on the surface. Light and images reflected on flat glass will be more recognizable and less distorted than the reflections on curved glass, which distorts images by virtue of its shape. For example, the curved lines of eyeglasses will make reflections that conform to the shape of the lenses.

Another notable property of curved glass is its tendency to reflect multiple highlights from one light source. As light shines on a water glass, for example, it is picked up at several points on the curve and becomes multiple stripes of highlights, some brighter than others. The image showing through the transparent glass is interrupted by the reflections.

Here is a summary of the major properties of glass and their effects on artists' renderings of it:

1. Glass reflects nearby colors and images. Curved glass will distort reflections by making them conform to its shape. Curved and uneven glass will reflect more than one highlight.

2. Since glass is transparent, colors and images behind the glass will show through. Curved glass will distort images more than flat glass.

3. The appearance of glass will be altered by its shape, color, thickness, and many other variables.

To learn how to draw glass, first choose one of the two categories, flat or curved, and find three photographs that show examples of that type. Draw from the photographs, using a tracing technique described in *Chapter two* or a freehand technique if you draw accurately. Begin with a black-and-white technique, and then try a color medium, like colored pencils or watercolors. At least one of the photographs you draw from should be in color.

Since there are many variations in glass within the flat and curved categories, you may have to select a subspecialty. For example, flat glass will look different if it is double-paned, if it is colored, or if it was made more than 50 years ago, when window glass was less pure and more distorting. Curved glass also comes in many shapes and sizes. If you are planning to make an illustration with an image of colored sunglasses, you should study three photographs of colored sunglasses, or some kind of colored, curved glass.

Once you have made three drawings of glass, make a fourth that combines the most distinctive elements of the preceding three as simply as possible without leaving out any of the characteristic qualities. Exaggerate the reflections and bright highlights, because they are the essence which makes it look shiny and "glasslike."

Making a simplified drawing will help you recognize the basic ingredients necessary in a particular illustration of glass. Reflections, highlights, and the transparent qualities of glass are what make it challenging to draw. If you can capture the essence, you will be able to portray glass using simple and complicated techniques alike with equal success.

HOW TO DRAW CHROME & OTHER SHINY METALS

Chrome and shiny metals reflect images like a mirror, but they also distort the reflections in conformance to the shape of the metal. For example, the curved chrome of a car bumper will reflect images that curve with the contour. The following properties of these metals affect the way you draw them:

1. They are highly reflective, mirroring nearby images and colors. Light sources shining on the metal will reflect as bright white highlights.

2. Images reflected in chrome will be distorted to the form of the metal.

3. The appearance of chrome and shiny metal will vary with differences in the color tint and shape.

Make a study by copying three photographs of chrome. Transfer the images from the photographs using a tracing technique described in *Chapter two* or draw them freehand. Use a black-and-white medium like pencils or ink wash, and then try a color medium like colored pencils or watercolors.

Make a fourth drawing of chrome that combines and simplifies the images sketched in the previous three drawings. This fourth drawing should capture the essence of chrome.

84 Artist: Richard Leech
Client: Yamaha
Media: Airbrushed watercolors
Richard Leech is a photorealist who paints more than can be found in a photograph. His brand of super-realism includes painting the inside and outside of an image all at once. This is an especially informative technique for showing the important working parts of a machine like the Yamaha motorbike. He also adds details and heightens the shine of the chrome and the paint.

Leech works a month a 60 hours a week to complete a detailed illustration such as this one for Yamaha. His dedicated nature and his respect for machines enable him to sustain such concentration. He has depicted machines of one kind or another since graduating from commercial art school in England. He worked as a technical illustrator for Rolls Royce and did illustrations for the first Lotus Elan brochure. Leech moved to the United States in 1963, and worked for Yamaha among others. He has illustrated other subjects, from kitchens to skyscrapers, but the subjects that stir his creativity most are machines.

DRAWING OTHER DIFFICULT SUBJECTS

The study you have been using to draw water, glass, and chrome is a research-and-practice approach which can be applied to any other subject that is difficult to draw—faces, hands, plastic objects, buildings, or any image which is particularly hard for *you*.

Here is a summary of the steps for drawing a problem subject:

1. Narrow the subject down to a specific category. For example, decide that you are going to study a "face in a frontal view" or "hands in a relaxed position."
2. Find three photographs of the difficult subject matter. If you plan to work in a color medium for this study, try to find color photographs.
3. Draw from the three photographs, making three drawings in a black-and-white or color medium. Work freehand or use a transfer or tracing technique from *Chapter two* to copy guidelines from the photographs. Copy all of the detail from the photographs.
4. Make a fourth drawing, combining the images from the preceding three simply without unnecessary details. In this drawing you will capture the essence of the subject.

This exercise encourages you to study the subject through photographs. Copying the subject three times from different photographs will acquaint your mind and hand with the shape, texture, and inherent abstract form of the subject. By the time you make a fourth drawing, you will know much more about it than when you began. The final drawing will be the most original since you will combine what you have learned from the three drawings and you will simplify the image as well.

Suggested Exercises

1. Make drawings of the subjects listed below that are simplified caricatures of the objects. The drawings should not necessarily be realistic or detailed, but they should communicate the subject instantly.
   - A sports car
   - A hamburger
   - A poodle
   - A light bulb turned on
   - A light bulb turned off

2. Make a study of water, choosing one category from the list in this chapter. Follow the study technique step by step. Use a black-and-white medium for the entire exercise.

3. Choose one of the titles below to make an illustration for a book cover.
   - *The Water We Drink*
   - *Waterfalls in North America*
   - *Waterfowl*
   - *The Seashore Vacation*

   Draw a thumbnail sketch and a rough drawing for the illustration. Make a study of water in the category that best fits the image of your illustration, using the study technique described in this chapter. Finish the illustration in a color medium such as colored pencils, pastels, or watercolors.

4. Make a study of glass from either category, flat or curved, using the study technique described in this chapter. Use a black-and-white medium for the entire exercise.

5. Make an illustration for a short story entitled one of the following:
   - "The Broken Window Mystery"
   - "Looking at Insects Through a Magnifying Glass"
   - "The Woman in the Rose-colored Glasses"
   - "The Glass Menagerie"

   Do a thumbnail sketch and a rough drawing for the illustration. Make a study of glass, choosing the category that best fits the image of your illustration. Use the study technique described in this chapter. Finish the illustration in a color medium such as colored pencils, pastels, or watercolors.

6. Make an illustration of a new car. Pick up a catalog of new models from a dealer for photographs to draw from. Use what you have learned about drawing glass, chrome, and shiny metal to make the car look brand-new and shiny.

7. Make a study of a subject that is especially hard for you. Choose any image except those which have been explored in this chapter. You might, for example, want to deal with faces, hands, feet, clothing, or buildings; the possibilities are limitless. Then narrow your subject to a specific like "faces from a frontal view." Use the study technique described for difficult subjects.

85 Artist: Brad Holland
Title: *The Seat of Power*
Media: Pen-and-ink

Brad Holland uses the most basic art technique, pen-and-ink, to produce complex, intriguing artwork. The complexity of the work is not in the technique, but in the idea behind it. Holland assembles images with a sensitive hand, creating illustrations that are felt as well as viewed. The sensations of seeing, hearing, and touching often inhabit Holland's work symbolically—multiple ears, eyes that are sewn shut, feet that appear to be hands. Using physical symbolism, Holland tells stories about the human condition, the illusions, dreams, and perceptions of people.

Except for the influence of a ninth-grade teacher who, he recalls, taught him the proportions of the human figure, Brad Holland learned to draw on his own. At age 17, he headed for Chicago with his drawings. After a detour working in a tattoo parlor, he found employment in an art studio and later success as a free-lance artist. Asked how he comes up with an idea, Holland says: "I rarely think it out. I just draw. It's like spirit-writing. I try to tap the nonverbal side of my brain. You know, only one side of the brain thinks in words. I try to tap that side, the animal instincts." (Quoted from *American Artist* interview by Nick Meglin)

Chapter
five
Special
Subjects

This chapter surveys some of the special subject categories of illustration. Some of these are based on a style, such as fantasy and surreal illustration, while others include a specific subject topic, such as people and portraits or product illustration. You will also find subject areas of professional specialties, for example, fashion and children's book illustration. Having previously covered the techniques of illustration, you are encouraged to specialize and further sharpen your skills in this chapter.

Fantasy & Surrealism

Fantasy and surrealistic illustrations are discussed as one since they have important qualities in common: both depart from a realistic representation of the world. It should be noted, however, that although the two schools have philosophical similarities, there are many different kinds and styles of both fantasy and surrealistic illustration. In general, fantasy and surreal illustration can be compared to poetry, while realistic styles of illustration are comparable to prose.

Prose must follow rules of grammar and be relatively straightforward to be understood, in the same way that realistic drawing and painting must adhere to the rules of how nature "looks." On the other hand, there are fewer rules governing poetry, and it is written in a wide variety of personal styles. Poetry may include slang, unfinished sentences, and disjoined phrases. If the poetry is good, it will communicate an idea or feeling because the poet has chosen the right words and

87

phrases intuitively. In the same way, fantasy and surreal illustration have fewer rules, and yet the images must be intuitively correct to be impressive. Many personal choices must be made in rendering a fantasy or surreal illustration, which account for the wide variety of differing interpretations of fantasy and surrealism.

Surrealism was the term used by French poet André Breton to describe a new literary and artistic movement in 1924. The most prominent surrealist of modern times is Salvador Dali (born in Spain in 1904), who painted *The Persistence of Memory,* one of the best-known surrealist paintings. In this painting, objects float, perspective is unnatural, and metal watches are limp and almost liquid. One watch hangs over a tree branch, while another drips over a corner wall, and a

86 Artist: Brad Holland
Title: *The Observation Deck*
Media: Pen-and-ink

87 Artist: Robert Steiner
Title: *Expulsion*
Published by: *Pomegranate*
Media: Pen-and-ink
Bob Steiner tests the limits of pen-and-ink techniques. Using a pen with a #000 tip, he characteristically makes lines so fine that they are barely visible to the eye. He builds up tone with a large vocabulary of different pen strokes, from crosshatching to invented textures, which give his work a wide range of values.

Steiner often draws from models or from photographs of his friends. He also makes use of nature books and photographic files in the library. In *Expulsion* he employed a composite of many different images to create a fantastic surreal scene. The artwork was meticulously planned and sketched lightly in pencil before he began to draw with a cartridge ink pen.

88 Artist: Robert Steiner
Detail of *Expulsion*

89 Artist: Marta Thoma
Client: *San Francisco Magazine*
Media: Watercolors

third hangs over an unknown object in the landscape. This kind of distortion is typical of surrealism. *Sur* in French means "beyond," so what we have is art that is "beyond reality."

The word *fantasy* encompasses the same territory as surrealism. It means "the realm of vivid imagination, illusion . . . make-believe . . . a disordered and weird image . . . (artwork) characterized by highly fanciful and supernatural elements. . . ." (Webster's New Collegiate Dictionary). There is a slight implication that fantasy artwork is a rearrangement of reality, while surrealism is a distortion of objects and reality. However, it becomes impossible to draw lines between these two approaches since they often occur at the same time to some degree. To simplify things, let us choose to interpret fantasy as an all-encompassing, blanket term for the qualities of both, so we can use a single term.

Have you ever looked at a fantasy illustration and wondered "how did the artist think of that?" The answer is not as mysterious as you may think. Let us see how a fantasy illustration is conceived by reviewing some of the different ways that images are manipulated to make them look unusual or surreal. As you read through these methods, keep in mind that an artist uses one method or another to fit the symbolism and mood of a particular illustration. Images are not made to look weird for no reason. Each image and the way it is manipulated are carefully chosen to express an idea. Be sure to read *Chapter four,* Communicating Your Idea, before you try any of the following techniques.

1. The size of an object is changed in relation to another. For example:
   - A very large hand reaching into a small house
   - A table with very tiny chairs around it
   - A large ant walking hand in hand with a person

The change in an object's size will be apparent only in comparison to another object. For example, let us say that you want to draw an airplane so that it looks very small. If you draw the small plane alone in the sky, its reduced size will only indicate that it is far away. If you add to the drawing a large figure holding a fly swatter, ready to hit the plane, the plane will appear to be unusually tiny. Or will the figure look like a giant? If other objects in the drawing look large, like the figure, the airplane will seem to be out of place. If, on the other hand, there is a small city below the figure, the figure will look like a

giant and the airplane will appear to be normal size.

2. The property of an object is changed. For example:
   - A metal watch is rubberlike.
   - A person floats weightlessly.
   - The sidewalk is sticky and gluey.

The properties most often changed are weight, solidity (objects melting), and texture.

3. Two subjects combine characteristics. For example:
   - A horse and a cloud combine in an image of a horse-shaped cloud in the sky.
   - A face and a candle combine in an image of a face melting like a candle.
   - A car and a wolf combine in an image of a vehicle with wolflike paws for wheels and a wolflike head and front grill.

This is a popular method of making a fantasy illustration. Subjects become half one thing and half another.

4. Subjects are found in an unnatural setting. For example:
   - A flower growing in a parking lot
   - A fish in a tree
   - A car in a house
   - A cow driving a motorcycle

This method is used most often for humorous illustrations, such as those in children's books. They are not disturbing or complicated images, like some created by the other methods; they are simply moved into an unnatural context. We have all seen children's book illustrations of animals dressed like humans eating, driving, shopping, and going about all the activities humans do. The animals look silly in human clothing, doing human things, and this is delightful to children.

90 Artist: Brad Holland
Media: Pen-and-ink

91 Artist: Marta Thoma
Client: St. Martin's Press
Media: Airbrushed and hand-painted
watercolors

92 Artist: Julian Allen
Title: *Weekend Voodoo*
Client: *Oui* magazine
Media: Acrylics and watercolors
Julian Allen is adept at a variety of different
art media, including watercolors, oils, acrylics,
and all of them in combination. Allen studied
art in England and in London as a free-lance
artist until 1973 when he was invited to work
under a six-month contract for *New York*
magazine; he worked for the magazine until
1977. Julian Allen is now a free-lance illustrator in New York City.

91

92

In one way or another all of these methods defy the rules of nature. The law of gravity may be defied, the properties of weight and mass altered, and so on. It may seem that the artists have completely turned their backs on reality, yet fantasy illustration depends on an element of realism to make it effective. For example, Dali's rubberlike watches are all the more incredible because, except for their shape, they are realistically rendered. Realism makes the fantasy more believable.

COLLAGE COMPOSITION TECHNIQUE #1

This is an excellent technique for learning how to make a fantasy illustration. After you are comfortable with it, try Collage Composition Technique #2 (which follows).

1. Choose a topic for an illustration. Let us say it is a book cover illustration (8½″ × 11″) for a book entitled *How to Interpret Your Dreams*.
2. Make a collage using pictures cut from old magazines to fit the book title. To keep it uncomplicated, do not use more than five pictures together in a collage. Rearrange the pictures in many different ways to find an interesting composition.
3. Use the collage as your rough drawing. Transfer the guidelines onto illustration board for the final artwork, using one

93

of the transfer techniques suggested in *Chapter two.*

4. Finish the illustration using either a black-and-white or color medium. Refer to your collage as you draw or paint the details of the artwork.

As you put the collage together, think about the four different methods of manipulating an image described in the preceding section. One or more of these methods can be used at the same time in your collage. Keep your idea simple to begin with, using two or three images in each collage. A collage can too easily become cluttered. A simple composition with symbolic impact can be as successful as complex work.

93 Artist: Fred Otnes
Title: *Europe Reborn*
Client: New American Library
Art Director: James Plumeri
Media: Collage and mixed media on linen
Fred Otnes uses many experimental techniques in his artwork. Inspired by American contemporary painting, he makes illustrations in collage or assemblage form. In the spirit of Rauschenburg, he does not limit his collages to cut paper photographs but uses many materials and often works in three dimensions.
   As a youth, Otnes worked in the art department of a newspaper where he became familiar with printing processes. Many of the techniques he uses today, like silkscreen, are derived from printmaking techniques.
   He often works on photosensitized linen which is mounted on a board. Using a vacuum frame to hold the linen board, he exposes negative photo images, which develop into positive images. Sometimes Otnes paints a background on the linen and he may paint an oil wash or airbrush on top of the photo images.
His assemblages feature a variety of materials such as wood, plaster, and photos, which are photographed with lighting that casts strong shadows and accentuates the dimensional quality.

There are two effective ways to use space when you make a collage: (1) as flat space on the picture plane or (2) as deep space receding from the picture plane. The flat space arrangement is more decorative and impressionistic. The deep space arrangement is more pictorial and surreal.

The most important rule for making a successful collage is that the images must be well integrated. In a flat space arrangement, the images may be related to each other by their individual designs or by the design they make together. In a deep space composition, the images must relate to each other to make the fantasy credible. This may be done by containing all the images in a central space like a landscape or a room or by having one image turn into another. To complete the fantasy composition you may need to add freehand drawing to the collage. Use your drawing skills to make the transition of one image to another, to add shadows and details, or other freehand work that improves the fantasy.

The extreme opposite of an integrated collage composition might be called the "patchwork quilt" type, and it should be avoided. A patchwork collage is made of randomly cut and pasted pictures which bear no relation to one another. Early on in school you may have learned to make collages this way, but for this particular exercise it will not work.

The elements of the collage should be glued or taped together and mounted in the correct dimensions of the finished illustration. Use graphite paper or a slide projection of the collage to transfer the guidelines onto the final art paper. (These techniques are described in *Chapter two.*) The guidelines should, as always, be transferred very lightly so they will not show through the final art medium.

A collage will quite naturally look fragmented since it is made from several pieces, but when you draw or paint the collage composition, the art medium itself will give unity to the illustration. Use the final medium to perfect the transitions from one image to another. The final picture should look like a believable fantasy, well integrated and unified.

COLLAGE COMPOSITION TECHNIQUE #2

This technique is more advanced and flexible than the preceding one. Instead of making an actual collage, the collage is pictured in your mind as you make a rough drawing. Because there is no need to cut up the pictures, many more sources of photographs can be used, such as library books and picture books. You can also add drawings from life and other freehand drawing. Because you can use many more sources in this technique, it is more likely that you can find images that fit your ideas instead of fitting your ideas to pictures in magazines.

1. Choose an illustration topic. Let us say that it is a book cover illustration (8½" × 11") for a book entitled *Improve Your Life through Hypnosis*.
2. Make a thumbnail sketch for the illustration using a fantasy composition. Refer to the four ways of manipulating an image for ideas (listed earlier in this chapter). Select the best sketch.
3. Look for source material that fits the images in the thumbnail sketch. Source material can be obtained from magazines, books, drawings from life, and drawings from your imagination.
4. Use your source material to make a rough drawing. Some of the photos may be traced. Smooth out any rough transitions between images.
5. Finish the artwork either in a black-and-white or a color medium. Refer to your source material as you draw or paint the artwork.

The first step in this technique requires that you visualize a fantasy scene, one or more for a thumbnail sketch. If you lack ideas, review the four methods of manipulating a fantasy image to spur your imagination. Keep in mind that image distortions should be symbolically consistent with the subject of the illustration.

Find source material that fits the images in your thumbnail sketch. Be as uncompromising as possible while you look for material at the library, in picture books, and in magazines. Drawings from life can be mixed with tracings from photographs or drawings from your imagination. Make a developed drawing from your thumbnail sketch and the source material. Transfer each image separately, using a tracing or freehand technique to make your rough drawing. Reduce or enlarge images to "fit" each other, carefully drawing the image freehand or with a copying machine, an opaque projector, or a slide projection machine.

Once again, keep in mind that the composition should be unified. Try this technique with only two or three images at first. Learn how to integrate a few successfully before you add more actors to the stage.

As you draw or paint the final artwork, the fantasy composition will be further unified by the overall texture of the medium. Refer to your original sources as you work on the final artwork to ensure accurate details.

Suggested Exercises

1. Examine a fantasy illustration in this book and answer the following questions:

   How many different images or elements are in the illustration?
   What possible source materials could the artist have used to draw the images?
   How are the transitions between one image and another handled?
   What type of space has been created, flat space or deep space?

   What methods have been employed to treat the subject as a fantasy?
   Have the size or proportions of an image changed?
   Have two subjects combined characteristics?
   Are the subjects in an unnatural place?

2. Make a fantasy illustration using Collage Composition Technique #1.
3. Make a fantasy illustration using Collage Composition Technique #2.

People & Portraits

Of all the subjects for illustrations, people and portraits are among the most captivating. It is our natural curiosity about others and ourselves that makes us look at a figure in a picture before anything else. Suppose you look at an illustration of a person standing in a room. Before you notice what color the room is and how many bookshelves there are, you will probably notice whether the person is male or female, young or old, attractive or unattractive, blond or bald. In addition, you will probably guess why the person is in the room from what he or she is doing.

People are especially interesting to each other because we are social animals and because we learn about ourselves from observing and interacting with others. Whenever you draw a figure for an illustration, viewers will try to identify with the person or think of people they know who are like that person. For example, let us say you draw an illustration of a dreamy-eyed woman holding a cat. Women looking at the illustration may have such thoughts as "she looks sad, just the way I feel sometimes" or "she is so pretty, I wish I looked like her" or "I like to hold my cat and sit and think like that, too." A man viewing the illustration may identify with the emotion or feeling surrounding the figure. He may have such thoughts as "I daydream like that sometimes" or "she looks a lot like my sister."

Men can identify with female figures, females can identify with male figures, blacks can identify with white figures—to an extent. Despite the natural and learned differences of sex and race, we share similar human emotions of love, hate, anger, aggression, and so on, which transcend other boundaries. However, there is no doubt that viewers will identify more completely with figures of their own sex and skin color. This is why the publishing business and television advertising have made an effort to include a fair amount of minority representation in textbook artwork and television commercials in the past few years.

The figures in children's books affect children's feelings about themselves. The

94 Artist: Burt Silverman
Client: *Time* magazine
Art Director: Walter Bernard
Media: Watercolors on board

Burt Silverman's career has spanned many years; his artwork has been seen on the cover of Time, in *The New York Times, Esquire, Newsweek,* and many other publications. The people he has painted have varied, as the characters in politics rise and fall, from Martin Luther King to China's Teng.

Silverman's portraits are more than a physical re-semblance; they capture the personality behind the portraits. He says of his work: "When I paint a por-trait, I try to be sensitive to the unique personality of that subject—and how it is revealed in their features and gestures." In order to be true to his subjects, Silverman rejects any formula approach. He says: "My techniques vary from illustration to illustration, depending on what I intuitively feel. Always the technique is at the service of the storytelling re-quirements of the picture. Each assignment has new problems and new solutions."

95 Artist: David Grove
Client: N.F.L. Properties
Art Director: David Boss
Media: Gouache and acrylics

David Grove begins an illustration by making a pencil rough drawing. Since his subject matter is often people or a figure, he photographs a hired model in the position that fits his concept. He takes color slides, which can be developed within 24 hours, and traces from the projected slide. The phototracing is combined with other images in a rough drawing.

Once the rough is approved, Grove begins the final artwork with an underpaint of gouache, applied in a painterly style which is very loose and sensual. He paints on top of the gouache with acrylics, bringing out details and emphasizing textures, faces, or other features of the painting.

Both of Grove's parents were artists, and he has enjoyed art from an early age. Since graduation from Syracuse University with a BFA in photography, he has pursued a career in art which has won him several honors from the Society of Illustrators.

female figures are examples and role models for little girls, as the male figures are for little boys. To give both boys and girls a chance to grow up without preconditioned sex-role stereotypes, most modern textbooks now try to represent both sexes as equally adventurous, intelligent, aggressive, thoughtful, caring, and so on.

What does all this mean to an illustrator? It means that people and portraits are very special subjects. They attract viewer attention more than any other subject, but in doing so, they also attract the viewer's critical eye, perhaps because the average person looks at him- or herself and others more closely than at any other subject.

Everyone is an expert on what a figure should look like, even those who cannot begin to draw one themselves. If an average viewer saw a doorknob off-center, it would probably go without comment. But if someone saw a nose off-center on a woman's face in your illustration, horrors! More than any other subject, a figure must "look right." This makes drawing people one of the most difficult of the artist's tasks, as well as one of the most rewarding.

DRAWING PEOPLE

A human figure can be illustrated in so many different ways that it is difficult to

describe them all. For example, a figure may be a small part of an illustration or it may take up the entire page, dominating the artwork. A figure may stand alone or interact with several figures. Figures may be old, small, young, fat, hunched, skinny, freckled, and so on. The possibilities are as infinite as your imagination. Let us begin to study this problem by describing three different elements that affect the way you draw a human figure.

1. Type of figure. This is the physical description of the figure, young or old, blond or brunette, pretty or plain, including the type of clothing the figure is wearing.

2. Position and action of the figure. This describes the way the figure is positioned in relation to the viewer—turned away, full face, three-quarter view—and any action the figure is performing—running, jumping, holding a glass of water, interacting with another figure in an embrace or handshake or fight, and so on.

96 Artist: John Collier
Client: American Journal of Nursing
Media: Pastels on paper

97 Artist: Burt Silverman
Client: *Fortune Magazine*
Art Director: Ron Campbell
Media: Watercolors
This illustration is a smorgasbord of different character types with a variety of expressions.

HOLLAND

3. Emotions of the figure. These can range from demonstrative, open displays of emotion, such as anger, happiness, or sadness, to mere hints of emotion, such as one would see in a stranger.

Here are some examples of the way a figure could be described in each category:

Figure type: young, cowboy-type, with hat and open shirt

Position and action: half torso, hands on hips, frontal position

Emotion: cool, neutral, direct eye contact

Figure type: little boy about eight years old, wearing oversized Superman T-shirt

Position and action: running fast

Emotion: happy, intent

Figure type: young woman dressed for winter

Position and action: ice skating, three-quarter view, back turned, hand touching behind back

Emotion: lonely, mysterious

98 Artist: Brad Holland
Title: *The Comedian*
Media: Pen-and-ink
Brad Holland had the following things to say about his portraits: "I make them up. You know, from spare parts. A mouth here, a nose or two there . . . Sometimes I begin with a model. But even then I try to imagine I'm that person. When I draw a forehead, I want to feel the weight of my own forehead. It's like acting. You can't just look at someone, otherwise it's you against them. You have to inhabit them. In the process, the drawing becomes a kind of self-portrait. A psychic self-portrait, anyway. Even in political drawings, no matter how much you might be gunning for someone, you can't forget to feel for them as people. Art always has to wear at least one of the faces of love. Otherwise it's just one more thing added to all the things in the universe." (From *American Artist* interview by Nick Miglen)

Before you draw a figure, describe the characteristics of the figure as you picture them in your mind. It may be helpful to write them down, as above. Once you have clarified the type of figure you want to draw, study it, following the techniques described in *Chapter four* under Drawing Difficult Subjects.

It is helpful to study figure drawing from books used in art classes. Many figure-drawing books and classes have students draw from a nude model, and any kind of experience like this will improve your skills, even if you never draw a nude for an illustration. The better you understand the human body, the easier it will be to draw nude or clothed figures.

If you would rather study the nude on your own or if you want to supplement what you have learned, you might buy a picture book of nude figures; the type sold in art stores is made especially for artists and illustrators. Such books have nude male and female models standing, walking, sitting, leaning, and in hundreds of other poses. You can draw from the pictures for practice. Later, you can refer to a book of poses when you are in need of a figure for an illustration. You can draw from the model, adding clothes and changing the model's features to fit your illustration.

The most contrasting textures on a figure are the skin, hair, and moistness of the eyes. All three of these parts of the body have a distinct, characteristic texture: one is smooth; one is stringy, stubbly, frizzy, or otherwise hairlike; and the third is wet.

People in Color. When you purchase paints, whether watercolors, oils, or acrylics, you will notice that there are no flesh-colored paints. Below is a list of the colors that can be used for painting flesh. Blending these paints in various combinations will produce every color of skin from the palest white to the deepest black.

• Burnt sienna
• Burnt umber
• Cadmium red
• Raw sienna
• Raw umber
• Violet
• Yellow ochre

When you are using an opaque medium, these colors will be mixed with white paint. Otherwise, they will be applied as washes or glazes which will allow the white of the paper to show through, except in the very darkest hues.

Many other colors can be used to paint skin, but the colors listed above are used most often in realistic figure painting. If you look at the skin on your own hand, you will notice that it is many different colors. Not only are there earth tones, pinks, a tinge of yellow perhaps, but you will also see the blues, violets, and greens of veins through the transparent flesh. For a very detailed, realistic painting, you would need to add green and blue to the above list. The painting *Portrait of Michael* on page 76 contains an example of flesh made up of many subtly blended colors.

A neutral earth color like burnt sienna is often used for a major part of the flesh, and other colors are added to provide shadows

Hans Albrecht Bethe

99

100

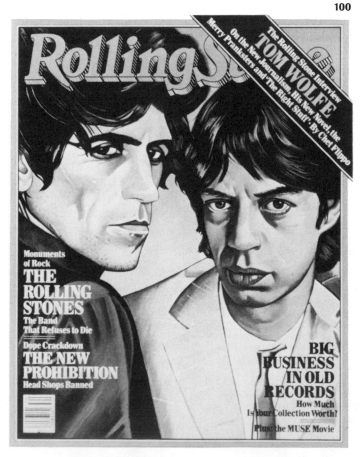

99 Artist: Burt Silverman
Client: *The New Yorker*
Art Director: Barbara Solonche
Media: Charcoal pencil

100 Artist: Julian Allen
Client: *Rolling Stone* magazine
Media: Oil paints

(a darker color such as burnt or raw umber), highlights (white paint or the white of the paper, pink in an area like a cheek), and reflected colors (red or violet). Lips, cheeks, the end of the nose, knuckles, and knees may be redder in color.

A figure in artificial light will have cooler looking skin colors than a figure in bright sunlight. Blues or violets may be used for shadows in artificial light. Bright sunlight brings out the red in flesh.

Earth colors such as burnt umber and raw umber are the starting points for brunette hair. To paint blond hair, try using yellow ochre and raw umber. The darker value can be used to make the shadows, and the yellow ochre can be used for the middle and light values.

THE PORTRAIT ILLUSTRATION

Portraits are a favorite and common subject for illustrations. There are two kinds of portraits, fictional and nonfictional. A fictional portrait is based on the description of a character in fiction, as interpreted by the artist. The nonfictional portrait depicts a real person. Politicians, musicians, movie stars, and astronauts are among the most popular subjects.

Drawing a person's likeness can be very challenging. Most of this section on portraiture deals with the problem of making a drawing or painting of a person that is true to life. However, some of the suggestions for bringing out the personality of a subject can be applied to fictional portraiture as well.

When you draw a portrait, you must capture the essence of the subject's personality in the same way you worked to capture the essence of inanimate objects in *Chapter four*. A portrait should be more than an exact physical likeness of the person; it should also reveal something about the subject's character. Let us look at some different ways to do this.

Some subjects are well known for their physical characteristics. Movie actors and politicians, in particular, groom themselves to emphasize such saleable physical traits as their attractiveness or their uniqueness. These features become an important part of their personalities, at least their public personalities, as they become well known for these features. The Nixon nose, the Kennedy hair, Dolly Parton's bust—these are examples of features that have become associated with the person. Characteristic features can also be more subtle, like the twinkle of an eye or the set of a chin. Cartoonists are experts at spotting unique, characteristic features of a person and exaggerating them in a caricature. In a portrait, these characteristics can be exaggerated as well, although perhaps more subtly.

Since it is unlikely that you will have a public figure in your living room for a day, you will have to rely on photographs of your subject as reference. Look for your subject in magazines from your own files or use back-dated magazines in the public library. The library is your best source, especially if your subject has been dead for some time or is only moderately well known.

Draw or trace your subject using one of the transferring methods described in *Chapter two*. Keep the distinctive features uppermost in your mind and emphasize these characteristics by exaggerating their size, color intensity, or some other property. A sharp nose may be drawn sharper, blue eyes made bluer, a tense face made more so. Downplaying one feature may serve to emphasize another: painting a face to look pale and colorless will make the blue eyes stand out.

There are many ways to bring out the subject's personality in a portrait. The person's activity may symbolize it, or the clothing, environment, or objects you include in the portrait will suggest something about an identity. Portrait painters have for centuries used symbols in order to reveal a subject's individuality. American folk art portrait painters often painted their subjects in front of a symbolic background, holding a symbolic object in their hands. A Navy officer might have been painted in uniform, holding a miniature ship in his hands while an ocean battle raged behind him framed in the window of his home. A young teacher might have been shown with a schoolhouse in the window behind her, holding a book in her hands. Priests inevitably hold Bibles.

However, symbolic imagery does not have to be blatant, and, in fact, there are many creative ways to integrate it in a portrait. There are many examples of this in the portrait illustrations included in this chapter.

Another way to vary a portrait is to use more than one image of the subject. A second or third image can show additional sides or facets of the person, symbolized by different moods or activities. There may be one central figure of the same size. If you choose this approach, you will have to work out an integrated design with the figures. (Refer to Fantasy and Surrealism earlier in this chapter for suggestions.)

MAKING A CARICATURE

A caricature and a portrait illustration have many things in common. In general, let us say that caricatures are simpler and more distorted than portraits in both image and technique.

Caricatures are, of course, well known for the way they exaggerate the characteristic features of a subject. A large nose, bushy eyebrows, or thick hair can be the key to instant recognition in a caricature so that there is no mistaking the identity of the subject. People with no particularly outstanding features are more difficult to caricature. The cartoonist must study them closely to discover subtle distinctions like the shape of the head or curl of the hair

THOMA

101

and concentrate on these unique details in the drawing.

To make a caricature, you will need to gather photographs of your subject to draw from. If you do not have a picture in your own file, you can find one among the back-dated magazines at the library. Draw a caricature freehand, if you are confident, or trace from a photograph, using an opaque projector, a homemade slide, or the graphite paper transfer technique discussed in *Chapter two*. Whether you trace or draw the subject, do not try to be accurate and stay on the lines of the original. Copy the contours of the face, making them larger or smaller depending on the feature you want to exaggerate. For example, if you are drawing the profile of a person with a very large, bulging

forehead, draw outside of the lines to exaggerate the forehead even more. If a person has a ski-jump nose, exaggerate this feature by increasing the curve of the ski-jump. Refer to the photograph to be sure that you are getting a likeness of the person. Study the shape and curves of the subject's head, ears, eyes, brow, nose,

101 Artist: Marta Thoma
Client: *San Francisco Chronicle*
Media: pen-and-ink

102 Artist: Edward Sorel
Client: *Harper's Magazine*
Media: Pen, ink, and watercolor

103 Artist: Burt Silverman
Client: *Time* magazine, International edition (unpublished)
Art Director: Arturo Casanēuve
Media: Watercolors

102

103

lips, jaw, hairline, and neck. The lines you draw for the caricature should imitate the shapes in the photograph, but change the proportions. Try different degrees of exaggeration as well, experimenting until you feel the caricature looks right.

Suggested Exercises

1. Make an illustration of one of the following subjects. Include from three to seven figures. Make a thumbnail sketch and rough drawing, and finish the illustration in a black-and-white medium.
   - A bus stop
   - A party
   - A business meeting
   - A hotel lobby
   - A movie ticket line

2. Make a fictional portrait or single-figure illustration of a character from a well-known fictional classic. Do a thumbnail sketch and a rough drawing. Here are some examples to choose from:
   - Huckleberry Finn
   - Tom Sawyer
   - Jane Eyre
   - Macbeth
   - Anna Karenina
   - Dr. Jekyll and Mr. Hyde

   Use a color medium to finish the illustration, referring to the People in Color section earlier in this chapter for paint choices.

3. Make a portrait of a well-known personality. Use the size dimensions 8½" × 11", and make a thumbnail sketch and a rough drawing for the illustration. Use one of the techniques suggested in this chapter to bring out the character of the subject. Finish the illustration in a color medium.

4. Make a caricature of a well-known personality. Use the size dimensions 6" × 6", and make a thumbnail sketch and a rough drawing for the illustration. Use pen-and-ink line work for the final art.

Product Illustration

Illustration is used together with photography and typography in the advertising business to sell and inform the public. Product illustration can be seen in newspapers, magazines, and brochures, and on billboards, packaging, and television. Just as there are many different approaches to advertising, there are many

104

105a   b

different kinds of product illustration, from simple, informational black-and-white to complex full-color artwork. Product illustration at its best can be as creative and exciting as any art form.

Typically, an artist is well paid for product illustration since businesses spend a great deal of money on advertising. The work is often higher paying than editorial illustration, for example, but there is a tradeoff with the degree of client control over the artwork. Since the success of a product often depends on how it is advertised and presented to the public, each step of an advertising campaign is carefully planned and evaluated for success. For an illustrator, this usually means that the conception and design will come from an agency art director to be made into a rough drawing and perhaps a more elaborate color rough drawing (a comprehensive) for the client's review. In an expensive advertising campaign, a

104 Artist: Doug Johnson
Client: Clark's Bar
Art Director: Preuit Holland
Doug Johnson's painting of a ''Clark's Bar'' is an example of realistic product illustration which is more convincing than a photograph. The candy bar is beyond realistic; it looks more than delicious and the wrapper looks more than new.

105a & b Artist: David Grove
Client: Pendleton Woolen Mills
Advertising Agency: Cunningham and Walsh
Art Director: Cal Anderson
Working drawing and finished artwork

rough drawing or comprehensive may be seen by as many as 15 people—from agency art directors, marketing directors, and account executives, to the agency's client—before it is finally approved. You can imagine the potential for differences of opinion as each person judges the artwork. If the artist is being well paid, he or she will be expected to make changes here and there to please the clients.

This process can be frustrating to the artist and art director as well because they must watch creative ideas be diluted by many changes and differences of opinion. The old saying "too many cooks spoil the broth" is applicable in advertising work. Artists and illustrators who want room to be creative should seek out a smart-thinking large company or a small graphic-design company, which will be minimally bureaucratic because of its size.

A good product illustrator will use communication skills and symbolism to enhance a product. (*Chapter four* discusses how symbols evoke emotions.) Advertising art directors are experts at using emotions to sell a product. You have surely seen an advertisement for a car which features a beautiful woman draped

106 Artist: Richard Leech
Client: Yamaha
Media: Airbrushed watercolors and pencil
Richard Leech paints a motorbike with greater detail and precision than a photograph could capture. "Photography," says Leech, "often makes the wheels of motorbikes look distorted. When I paint a bike, the wheels look more perfectly round." In a photograph, black parts of the machine are often indistinguishable from other black parts. Using an airbrush, Leech can paint each of these areas with definition and precision. He paints chrome to look even more shinier and enhances the textures of leather and paint. He is also able to show the working parts of the motor in position on the body of the bike.

Understandably, Leech's work is often mistaken as a photo. An art director who once saw Leech's work partly finished, half airbrushed and half in pencil, decided to reproduce it as it was. He felt that the illustration in this stage highlighted the important parts of the bike and yet looked more obviously like a piece of painted art.

seductively on the product. This is supposed to suggest that a man purchasing the car will attract beautiful women to him. A woman viewing the advertisement may picture herself becoming that beautiful figure if she purchases the car. The advertising has associated the car with sex, a powerful motivation loaded with emotion.

Whether it is right or good to sell a car this way is another discussion altogether. From the company's point of view, it is natural to want to show a product in the most pleasing way. On the other hand, when a product is basically useless or harmful, like cigarettes, it may be distasteful to see it associated with a positive human emotion like love.

There are two technical approaches to making a product illustration "realistic" and "interpretive." They can be used separately and in combination.

REALISTIC
PRODUCT ILLUSTRATION

A product illustrator is often asked to draw or paint a product so that it looks realistic, and there are many good reasons for doing so. To begin with, the purpose of product illustration is to be informational. For products such as cars, clothes, and furniture that sell to a large extent on the basis of looks, an illustration must be accurately representational. The manufacturer of technical products, such as machinery or computers, may want to show the functional details that make them desirable and saleable. Finally, the look of a product sets it apart from its competitors.

If it is advantageous to portray a product

realistically, why not use photography for all product advertising? After all, a camera can record an accurate image. The answer is that illustration can do things that a camera cannot. For example, an illustration can:

1. Include details that would not show up well in a photograph.
2. Be more precise and clear in detail than a photograph.
3. Combine realism with surrealism or fantasy for an interesting advertisement (see the following section, Interpretive Product Illustration).
4. Exaggerate the attractiveness or newness of a product.

To make a realistic illustration, it is necessary to have either the product or photographs of it before you. The techniques described in the section on photography (*Chapter one*) can be useful in making a product illustration. Transferring or tracing from a photograph with one of these techniques will start you off with correct proportions and an accurate drawing.

Draw from both the product and photographs if your assignment requires an emphasis on detail. You can trace the correct proportions from the photograph and refer to the actual product for details.

Every product has specific characteristics that are central to its appeal. Thus there are many ways to emphasize a product's attractiveness. The appeal of a sports car may be in its shape and the way it handles on the road. In this case, an illustration would emphasize the lines and the roadworthiness of the car, perhaps by showing it speeding along a twisting coastal highway. The newness would be emphasized by the sparkle of its windows and chrome and by the crisp reflections in

the paint. (Refer to Drawing Difficult Subjects in *Chapter four* for suggestions on drawing glass and chrome.)

Here are some examples of other products and the characteristics that make them appealing. These are the features that should be emphasized in a product illustration.

Fur coat: luxuriousness of texture and design

Lawn mower: functional details

Sofa: design, styling, and comfort

Pots and pans: newness, shine, shape, and design

Motorboat: newness, shine, shape, design, and power of motor

An artist who excels at technique will do well in product illustration, but mastering technique takes a lot of practice. Begin by trying all of the different ones discussed in this book. Then choose the medium you like best and specialize. Any of the mediums discussed in this book can be used for product illustration, from acrylics to watercolors, inks, airbrushed acrylics, and oil paints. Suppose, after experimenting with several, you find that you like painting acrylics with an airbrush more than any other technique. Practice that skill over and over until you acquire expertise, because it takes skill and control to render a product realistically.

107 Artist: Bruce Wolfe
Client: Yellowstone Bourbon
Art Directors: Bill Berenter/Stuart Bresner
Media: Casein underpainting with oils
This illustration demonstrates a way to accommodate a substantial area of type on artwork. The lower left-hand area is less busy and lighter in color so that the type can be easily read. If you plan an illustration with type, consider these general rules:
1. The area (the size of the type) should not be overly busy.
2. The color of the area should create contrast with the type color. A light area contrasts well with black type, a dark or black area will contrast well with white (or negative) type, and so on.

INTERPRETIVE PRODUCT ILLUSTRATION

An interpretive product illustration is more than a realistic drawing or painting of the product. It emphasizes usefulness, attractiveness, or other saleable qualities by creating a scene with other images in the illustration. Here are some of the ways that this can be done:

1. *Show the product being used.* A product that sells because of its efficiency and performance is a good candidate for this method. Examples might be a motorcycle, tennis racquet, lawn mower, copy machine, or lounge chair.
2. *Show the results of using a product.* Some products, like shampoo, are bought because of what they promise to do. Since the result of using shampoo will be clean hair, an interpretive shampoo illustration would include an image of a woman or man with shiny, fluffy hair. Other examples of products and their results are:
   • Insecticide—dead bugs
   • Dishwashing liquid—clean dishes
   • Perfume—attracts the opposite sex
   • Vitamins—healthy body
3. *Create a mood or environment that enhances the product.* An interpretive technique might use a painting of an airplane flying through beautiful clouds or a camper parked beside a fishing stream to associate the experience of flying or owning a camper with feelings of serenity. A mood can also be created with a fantasy technique (see Fantasy and Surrealism earlier in this chapter).

Whatever method is used, it is almost always necessary for the product itself to be identifiable and realistic, even if other images in the illustration are not. Take, for example, the illustration I made for Footgear, which advertises men's leather boots and shoes. In an unusual swamp setting, alligators are modeling the shoes. The alligators and the scene look highly fanciful, but the shoes themselves are rendered realistically, down to the last seam.

In rare cases, a product or company may be so familiar to the public that a specific image of the product may not be necessary in the advertisement. A large oil company, for example, may want to depict the many different ways its product is used, from making rubber balls to heating homes. In this case, there is no single product to portray, and the artist is asked to illustrate an idea, as is done in editorial illustration. The purpose is to create a positive image about the large company, rather than to try to sell a specific item. The illustration by Paul Pratchenko for Boise-Cascade is an example (see Color Plate II). The artwork itself is beautiful and imaginative, which reflects well on Boise-Cascade, a paper company. There is no obvious product being sold, but the viewer willingly reflects on the intriguing artwork with its images of paper and the source of paper, the forest.

Suggested Exercises

1. Make a simple, realistic product illustration for a hypothetical newspaper advertisement. Use pen-and-ink and ink wash. Choose one of the following subjects.
   • A sofa advertisement
   • A blue jeans advertisement
   • A shoe sale
   • A hotel advertisement
   Use a photograph of the subject to help make your illustration.
2. Make a realistic illustration for a new car advertisement. Visit a car dealership to obtain photographs to work from. (Car dealers hand out free brochures.) Make a rough drawing for the illustration, then make the finished artwork in a color medium.
3. Make an interpretive product illustration for a hypothetical brand of running shoes. Make a rough drawing for the illustration, then complete the illustration with a color medium.
4. Make an interpretive product illustration for a hypothetical brand of hand lotion. Make a rough drawing for the illustration, then complete the illustration using a color medium.

Fashion Illustration

Other Sections to Study
• *Drawing and Composition (Chapter one)*

Fashion illustration is the art of illustrating clothes and accessories. It is a kind of specialized product illustration, with the purpose of advertising clothes for retail outlets and clothes designers.

For many years, fashion illustration was taught and practiced in the same way: the figure was made to look elegant and slightly stylized, and the technique used most often was pen-and-ink with ink wash. So, for years artwork for fashion illustration held few surprises. But since about the mid-1970s, we have seen

• *Illustration Techniques (Chapter two, Chapter three)*
• *Communicating Your Idea (Chapter four)*
• *Fantasy and Surrealism, People and Portraits, Product Illustration (Chapter five)*

innovations galore. Fashion illustration has become more experimental in style and technique, to the extent that we now see some figures rendered realistically, in a style approaching photorealism. The environment around the figure has become more important as artists attempt to create a mood or feeling about their drawings, and it may take the form of a

108 Artist: George Stavrinos
Client: Bergdorf/Goodman
Media: Drawing media
In this illustration for a velvet jacket designed by Giorgio Armani, Stavrinos creates a fantasy environment with a variety of textured images. The crinkled paper backdrop being pulled aside by the figure suggests the texture of crinkled fabric and, in particular, of crinkled velvet in a clever, almost tongue-in-cheek manner.

109 Artist: George Stavrinos
Client: Bergdorf/Goodman
Media: Drawing media
The geometric shape of this design by Halston is enhanced by a geometric environment. The dress and pants fall in a long line like a Roman column. Architectural shapes on two sides of the figure echo the geometry. Mysterious clouds and shadows behind the figure create a mood of intrigue and elegance.

George Stavrinos, who regularly creates advertisements that appear in *Vogue*, has revitalized fashion illustration with a unique style and photorealist technique that lends a new look. He adds yet another dimension by creating a conceptual or environmental element inspired by the design of the clothes.

fantasy or surreal environment. Artists are also experimenting with active figures and unusual poses. All of this adds up to artwork that is branching out in many directions and making the field of fashion illustration more vital.

A professional illustrator draws from a live model or, more often, from a Polaroid snapshot of a model wearing clothes provided by his or her client. It is more convenient and economical to hire a model and take photographs than to take up hours of the model's time drawing from life. To be able to draw skillfully from the photographs, a fashion illustrator has typically studied drawing, and life drawing in particular.

Most fashion illustration is reproduced in black and white in newspapers and magazines. For this reason, illustrators work primarily with black-and-white mediums, such as pen-and-ink, ink wash, pencils, charcoal, crayons, and paints. The technique must be applied boldly if it is to be reproduced on newsprint, since small details can get lost. Any of the color mediums described in *Chapter three* can be used when the occasion arises for a color advertisement.

The design of the garment or accessory will determine what the artist emphasizes. Mia Carpenter, a fashion illustrator in Los Angeles, says that ''certain fashion designs tend to bring out certain artistic interpretations.'' Here are some of the ways an artist may choose to be interpretive:

1. Exaggerate what is interesting about the garment—for example, lines, curves, texture.
2. Exaggerate the figure's interesting characteristics or proportions—for example, the model's height, width, curves, curly hair.
3. Allow the model to reflect a mood by the way you draw his or her posture, attitude, action or inaction.
4. Create a mood in the environment—for example, by the way models are interacting; by drawing a background scene, such as a landscape, urban scene, science fiction fantasy; by including props or objects like flowers in the model's hands; or by showing action, such as tossing a ball.

Whatever is most enhancing and appropriate to the garment and garment design should be the basis of your interpretation.

Suggested Exercises

1. Do three fashion illustrations, using a black-and-white medium and drawing from a fashion photograph such as you might find in *Vogue* or *Harper's Bazaar*.
   • Make one drawing very realistic with with realistic proportions.
   • Make one drawing stylized, exaggerating the features of the model.

   • Make on drawing in a stylized or realistic technique and create an environment for it. Do not use the environment in the photograph, but make up a new one. If necessary, you can consult another photo as a reference for the background.

2. Ask a friend or hire a model to pose for a few snapshots. Dress the model

in something simple, like a bikini. Use the snapshots to draw a fashion illustration, 8″ × 8″. Make a rough drawing for the illustration, and then complete it in a black-and-white medium.

Children's Book Illustration

Other Sections to Study
- *Drawing and Composition (Chapter one)*
- *Illustration Techniques (Chapter two, Chapter three)*
- *Communication (Chapter four)*
- *Fantasy and Surrealism, People and Portraits (Chapter five)*

Over the years, many artists have been attracted to the field of children's books. Classics like Beatrix Potter's illustrations for *Peter Rabbit* and Sir John Tenniel's for *Alice in Wonderland* are reprinted year after year and cherished for generations. Subjects in children's books have traditionally been rich with creative imagery for the artist. Mad hatters, talking rabbits, and a prince who visits from outer space are just a few of the "ordinary" people in children's books.

An artist who is interested in drawing for children will naturally find inspiration in personal childhood experience. Dealing with imaginary monsters, making friends, pleasing and not pleasing parents,

learning new skills every day—these are just a few of the experiences of childhood that can be inspirational if the artist can remember them. Contact with young children may help to revitalize the memories.

A warm, personal touch is a prerequisite for good children's book illustration. The artwork must communicate in an expressive manner either by personalizing the characters and subject matter or by using expressive colors or brushstrokes. A cold, mechanical technique or an impersonal approach to the subject matter will not go over well with children. For this reason, techniques like photorealism or slick airbrushed illustrations are rarely seen in children's books. Children demand something more personal. A children's book illustrator must put aside all personal reserve to reach the audience, the way we will make a funny face and look foolish to a child to make him or her laugh. Marcia Brown, a children's illustrator and book critic, describes it in this way: "Many artists are copying photographs of action shots of athletes, children in motion and animals that they can hardly hope to find as models. Some have enough life behind their pens to bring the child copied to new life on the page; others simply do not, and we are left

110 Artist: Arnold Lobel
Title: *The Darkling Elves*
This illustration appeared in *The Headless Horseman Rides Tonight* by Jack Prelutsky. Illustration copyright © 1980 by Arnold Lobel. Reprinted by permission of Greenwillow Books (A division of William Morrow & Company).

111 Artist: John Tenniel
Title: *Jabberwocky*
This illustration appeared in an 1865 edition of Lewis Carroll's famous book *Through the Looking Glass*.

with seams in trousers and wrinkles in sleeves instead of a person."

ARTWORK FOR DIFFERENT AGE LEVELS

The requirements for children's art change with the age of the group for whom the literature and art are intended. The preschool child enjoys picture books that have very simple words or no words at all to accompany the artwork. As the child grows older, storybooks become more involved, and the pictures reflect the advancing maturity.

This makes it vital for the artist to know and understand the age group which is to be captured. It is helpful to be able to draw children who look the age of your readers, since there is often, but not always, a central character for the children to identify with. Children's proportions change as they grow older; younger children have chubby proportions and a head that is relatively large in comparison to the rest of the body. As they grow, they become taller and thinner, but the size of their heads changes only slightly. It would be good preliminary exercise to make a study of the age group you are interested in, sketching the children from life and from photographs. Include sketches of the children engaged in activities typical of their age. For example:

Three- to four-year-olds: playing with dog, tossing ball, getting dressed

Six- to eight-year-olds: riding bicycle, climbing tree, walking to school, flying a kite

Teenagers: talking in a group, driving a car, playing football

These are just a few suggestions to give you an idea of how to begin. You might also reread Drawing Difficult Subjects in *Chapter four* and apply the method suggested there to a particular age group.

The artwork in picture books for younger children, from three to eight years old, tells most or much of the story, so the artist is responsible for advancing the action and excitement. If you look through a book illustrated by Maurice Sendak, you can see how the pictures carry the story line from one page to the next in a gradual but compelling way.

Because picture books require an abundance of illustration and the reproduction costs can be quite high, the artwork is rarely reproduced in four-color throughout. Pen-and-ink line work is very popular for children's books, and a second or third color is often added with handcut or simply prepared stencils. (See The Simple Line Drawing and Variations in *Chapter two.*)

Suggested Exercises

1. Make an illustration 6" × 6" for a familiar nursery rhyme. Do a rough drawing and use pen-and-ink line techniques for the finished artwork.
2. Make an illustration 8" (width) × 10" (depth) for a familiar fairy tale. Do a rough drawing and use a color medium for the finished artwork.
3. Write a short children's story. The following are suggestions for a story line:

- Use a child or an animal as the main character.
- Create a difficult situation or make up a problem and have the character find a solution. (Examples of problems would be a boring afternoon, too many guests in one room, a long hot walk, making a new friend, a ghost in the closet.) Make two or three 6″ × 6″

illustrations for your short story. Do a rough drawing, and use pen-and-ink line techniques to finish the artwork. The illustrations should include the following:
- A sense of action.
- Expression of different emotions by the main character. Use your own face in the mirror as a model for expressions.

Technical Illustration

Other Sections to Study
- *Drawing and Composition (Chapter one)*
- *Illustration Techniques (Chapter two, Chapter three)*
- *Communicating Your Idea (Chapter four)*
- *Graphic design, paste-up, drafting (not included in this book)*

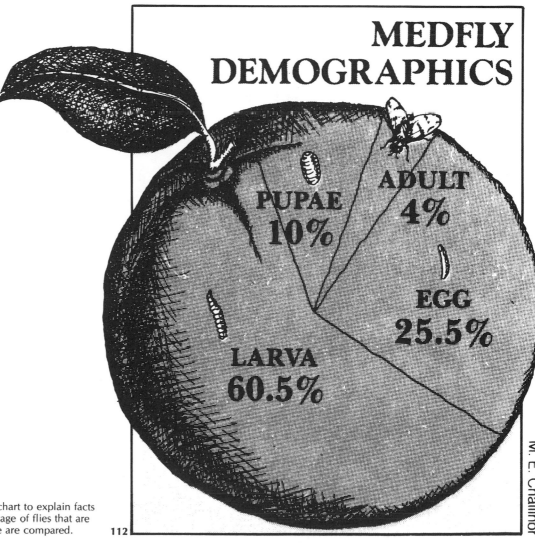

Artist: M. E. Challinor
Client: *Science 82* magazine
An orange is made into a pie chart to explain facts about the fruit fly. The percentage of flies that are adults, eggs, larvae, and pupae are compared.

M. E. Challinor

Technical illustration is the art of illustrating facts and figures. It is used abundantly in how-to manuals and in publications on such subjects as science, math, and business to illustrate factual information. There are many different varieties of technical illustration, but most can be described as diagrams, charts, and graphs.

In visual form, the relationship of facts and figures to each other can become clearer. For example, a diagram of the anatomy of the human eye can show where the iris is located in relation to the retina and the other parts of the eye in a fraction of the time it would take to explain in words. On a chart of figures, like a population chart of major American cities, you see at a glance which cities are the largest and by what proportion. Of course, the success of a technical illustration depends on the artist's ability to translate facts into a clear, precise, interesting graphic form. Each assignment has its particular requirements and challenges.

Many technical illustrators have some background in math and drafting. Competence in math is handy whenever you are working with proportions in a chart that must be visually correct. For example, let us say you are given the information that Company A sells 100,000 cars per year and Company B sells 150,000 cars per year. To make it interesting, you have decided to represent each company as a car, enlarging Car B to show that it represents more sales. Exactly how much larger than Car A should Car B appear? It should be half-again the size of Car A, if you know your math.

A knowledge of drafting is invaluable to the technical illustrator since many of the skills are the same. Line work is often used in technical illustration, and a draftsman is taught to make a controlled, even line with pencil or pen. A draftsman works on graph paper, using instruments like the T-square, triangle, and ruler to make precision drawings, and these same techniques and materials are used by the technical illustrator. For a black-and-white chart or graph, the illustrator will use drafting paper because the light-blue lines of the grid will not show up in reproduction. The artist will also use a triangle and ruler to achieve the precision of a draftsman.

Templates are another tool used in both drafting and technical illustration. They are plastic stencils sold in various sizes and shapes, as circles, rectangles, ellipses, arrows, and stars. Tracing around the inside of the stencil is a fast way to make accurate geometrical shapes. Used cleverly, template shapes can be fashioned into figurative images. For example, a rectangle can be easily made to look like a dollar bill to illustrate a piece on money.

The study of lettering, type, and paste-up is a must for the technical illustrator. The typeface chosen must be easy to read and appropriate to the style of the subject matter. Press-on or cold type is often used in this field because hot metal type smears too easily.

Many times a screen or pattern is chosen from the Format or Zipatone product lines to add tone to an illustration. These are plastic sheets of patterns printed in varying densities which can be placed on the line drawing or on an overlay. (These instant tone methods are discussed in more detail in *Chapter two*.) For technical illustration, they can be a fast, appropriate method of creating different values.

A technical illustration can be interesting as well as clear and precise. One way to incorporate interest is to weave figurative images of the subject matter into the illustration. For example, in a bar graph, (1) if the subject matter is money, the bars could be dollar bills, (2) if the subject is death, the bars could be tombstones, and (3) if the subject is alcohol, the bars could be bottles, and so on. Or, let us say that the facts you are illustrating are "where the money from record company sales goes." This is a case of a total sum being divided into parts—a perfect candidate for a pie chart. However, instead of leaving it as a simple circle, to fit the subject matter, why not make the chart look like a record? The image of the record can also be divided to represent the percentages.

There are many different ways to add interest by making the technical illustration more figurative. The rules to remember are: (1) be sure it is appropriate to the subject matter and (2) draw the figurative images simply and clearly so that they provide enjoyment without interfering with the information.

Another way to enliven a simple chart or graph is to give it a third dimension by showing the side, bottom, or top of images like the bars in a bar graph. Often a side view is combined with a top or bottom view and shaded or filled in with black to give the image the illusion of casting a shadow. This is called adding a "drop shadow." The effect is to make the image, whether it is a bar, an arrow, or a dollar bill, jump forward and appear to be three-dimensional.

Lawrence Peterson, a technical illustrator in Palo Alto, California, says of his artwork, "A good technical illustration is one which catches the eye of the reader and then conveys the information accurately. The illustration should always be made to suit the subject. The creative part is how the lines and values are executed and the way you present the relationships of the facts and figures."

Suggested books on the subject of technical illustration include *The Design of Books* and *Editing by Design* (see *Bibliography*).

Suggested Exercises

1. Make a three-step technical illustration which shows one of the following as it might appear in a how-to book:
   • Thread a needle
   • Change a flat tire
   • Change a light bulb
   Make each step of the illustration finished size, 3″ × 3″, and use pen-and-ink line work only.
2. Make a 6″ × 6″ technical illustration, using the following information about how much alcohol it takes to make a 160-pound person legally drunk:
   • 6 beers (10 ounces each)
   • 15 ounces of fortified wine
   • 24 ounces of table wine
   • 6 glasses of liquor

3. Make a pie chart 6″ × 6″, using the following information:
   • 40 percent registered Democrats
   • 32 percent registered Republicans
   • 20 percent Independent
   • 8 percent undecided

Medical Illustration

Other Sections to Study

• *Drawing and Composition (Chapter one)*
• *Illustration Techniques (Chapter two, Chapter three)*
• *Communicating Your Idea (Chapter four)*
• *Technical Illustration, People and Portraits (Chapter five)*

A medical illustrator combines the talent of an artist with a knowledge of scientific facts. A typical graduate program for medical illustration includes the study of anatomy, pathology (study of disease), histology (microscopic study of cells), human physiology (how the parts of the body function), human embryology (growth and development of the fetus), and neuroanatomy (the anatomy of the nervous system), as well as art and design. A career in medical illustration should appeal to a person who is attracted to the fields of both art and science. As a freelance medical illustrator told me about her career, "I feel lucky to have been able to narrow my career choices down to two fields of study—art and science—instead of one. I have enjoyed learning the fascinating facts about science while using my career skills."

Medical illustration demands a depth of scientific knowledge best learned in a graduate medical illustration program. Most programs are affiliated with a medical school and require two to three years to complete. Entry into the programs is highly competitive; typically, schools accept only three to eight new students per year. Students are expected to have an undergraduate degree in either art or the life sciences, and they are asked to submit a portfolio of artwork for review.

Art courses taught in a medical illustration program include life drawing from models, drawing, painting, and design skills. A medical illustrator must learn to draw with extreme accuracy and realism and to reduce a complex idea to a simple explanatory diagram or schematic concept.

The advance of modern medicine and technology has changed medical illustration. Until recently, artwork was used almost exclusively in medical publications. However, technical advances in photography have greatly increased its use in medical illustration. Now that the camera can delete unimportant information and emphasize important information, photography is often used instead of artwork because it is more practical or economical.

Traditionally employed to draw for publications, medical illustrators are now asked to work in a variety of communications media, from slide presentations to movies, videotapes, videocassettes, and closed-circuit TV. Fast-breaking medical developments demand an instantaneous communication medium. Research discoveries that could take six months to a year to publish in a journal can be shared more quickly through an audiovisual medium.

113 Artist: Gerald P. Hodge
Title: Tumor of the pancreas
Client: Norman W. Thompson, M.D.; Dept. of Surgery, The University of Michigan
Technique: Pen-and-ink on scratchboard

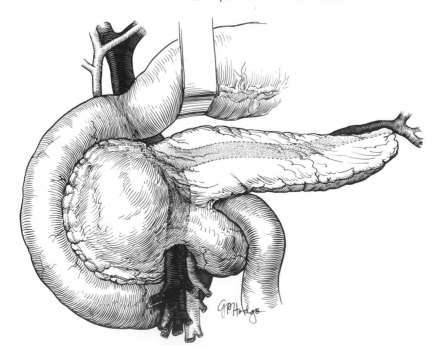

The style of the artwork must change to suit the medium for which it is made. The trend is toward a diagrammatic style of drawing that is highly conceptual, partly because artwork made for an audiovisual presentation is typically more diagrammatic than realistic and partly because diagrammatic drawings are faster and less expensive. This style of medical illustration is flourishing.

At the same time, medical illustration is finding new expression for traditional forms like textbooks and brochures. As the field becomes more diversified, part of the creativity involved will be matching the style or technique of the art to the media and the particular assignment. (*Chapter four* is especially relevant to this issue.)

For more information about graduate medical illustration programs, write to the Association of Medical Illustrators, 5820 Wilshire Boulevard, #500, Los Angeles, California 90036, or phone (213) 937-5514.

Architectural & Mechanical Illustration

Other Sections to Study

- *Drawing and Composition (Chapter one)*
- *Illustration Techniques (Chapter two, Chapter three)*
- *Communicating Your Idea (Chapter four)*
- *Product Illustration (Chapter five)*
- *Drafting (not included in this book)*

Architectural and mechanical illustration are closely related to their fields of specialization—architecture and engineering. Courses of study in these areas always include drawing and drafting classes as a means of conceptualizing designs. The architectural or mechanical engineering student who enjoys drawing more than the actual designing of buildings or machines will naturally be attracted to a profession in specialized illustration.

Both of these fields of illustration require drafting and drawing talents. Drafting classes teach a student how to interpret and draw from blueprints. An architectural illustrator is expected to be able to draw a building as it will look by interpreting his or her own or another architect's blueprint design for a building. In the same way, a mechanical illustrator must be able to draw a machine as it will look, in the correct proportions, by reading the blueprint design for the machine.

Each field contains particular subject matter at which an artist must become proficient. For the architectural illustrator, this means learning to draw the different materials used for the construction of buildings as well as the landscape around them: stucco, wood paneling, glass, metal, cement, rock, brick, tile, asphalt, shrubs, trees, and ground covering. Each material has a unique texture that must be drawn convincingly. When figures are added to the illustration, they too must be the correct size in relation to the size of the building.

Mechanical illustration is used to conceptualize products in the process of being developed. The illustrations allow engineers and designers to evaluate their products before they are placed on the market.

The subjects encompass a wide variety of machines and products, such as cars, car engines, traffic lights, drawbridges, hair dryers, or microcomputers. To render them convincingly, an illustrator must be skilled at drawing the textures of industrial products like plastic, glass, mylar, chrome, and rubber.

114

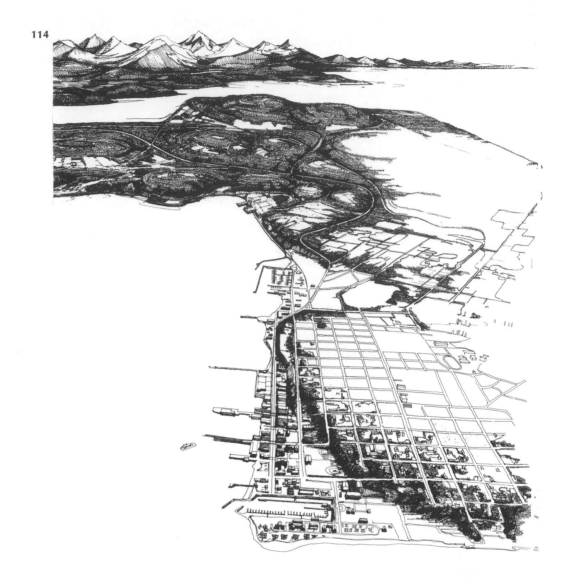

115

114 Artist: James Pettinari
Media: Rapidograph pen with a #000 tip
One way to make topographic illustration more interesting than a map is to give it perspective and render the more interesting or important features. How can you make aerial drawings in the correct perspective without paying a pilot to fly you over the area for pictures? One way is to take photos of a flat map (or curved globe) from various angles, as if the camera were an airplane flying over. With the camera at an angle, a map will photograph as if it is a landscape. The photo can be used to trace the correct placement of the geographic features. In this illustration, the mountains along the coast are emphasized more than the interior landscape to highlight the topic of the architectural study. The mountains in the distance enhance the illusion of space.

115 Artist: James Pettinari
Media: Rapidograph pen with a #000 tip
This illustration is one of a series made for a waterfront study of the city of Port Townsend, Oregon. In this drawing, James Pettinari chose to emphasize the image of water and the architecture of the city's water edge. To capture the head-on view of the waterfront, the artist took several telephoto pictures as he approached the city in an ocean ferry. From several photos, he composed one long detailed illustration.

116 Artist: Marta Thoma
Title: *Reaching for the Moon*
Media: Watercolors

Chapter
six
Illustration
as a Profession

An illustrator can work for him- or herself on a free-lance basis or can work in an agency or company for a salary. Not many companies hire full-time illustrators; more often they hire artists who have a combination of skills in design, paste-up, and illustration. If you are interested in working full-time for an agency or company, it is a good idea to learn paste-up, design, and the printing process, as well as illustration.

A freelance illustrator must be his or her own salesperson to get started. Once established with a few jobs, the freelancer may seek an agent to be his or her representative. An agent usually represents several artists at one time, finding clients and work for them. Some artists prefer not to have an agent because agents take about 25 percent of the fee for any job they find for their clients. However, an agent can be very useful to the shy artist, the extremely busy artist, or the artist who does not live in a large city.

Preparing a Portfolio

An artist's portfolio is his or her ticket to finding work. The first portfolio will be filled with student artwork. This book contains many exercises that give you the opportunity to start building a portfolio. If you have followed the book through, step by step, you have completed several student illustrations that are likely candidates for a portfolio. Choose the best among them for inclusion.

The most practical kind of portfolio to buy is one that has protective plastic-covered loose-leaf pages which display your artwork. Choose one big enough to hold your largest illustration. A portfolio will cost $20 or more, but it is worth the investment. It is a professional way to present your work because it creates a neat, uniform appearance. Clients who are in a hurry can quickly flip through the pages. The plastic protects your artwork from fingerprints and the abuse of repeated handling.

If you do not want to buy a portfolio, each illustration should be either matted or mounted with a protective overlay and presented as neatly as possible, wrapped in clean paper. A clean, neat, professional presentation that reflects well on the artist cannot be overemphasized. It says to a client that you are capable of delivering artwork for a job in a similar way. Student illustrations should never look dirty or worn from handling.

Choose 10 to 15 of your best studies for the portfolio. It is better to have fewer pieces than to display some that are not technically well done. Vary the subject matter in the illustrations; include objects, people, products, scenes. Do include subjects you are especially interested in. If you would like to illustrate children's stories, be sure to have illustrations of children in your portfolio. If there are particular subjects you do not enjoy, for example, technical illustration, do not put any samples in with your work. Some clients will hire an artist only if they see exactly what they have in mind in the portfolio. It is best to include examples in black and white as well as in color.

To sum up suggestions for a good portfolio:

1. Choose 10 to 15 pieces of art.
2. Quality is better than quantity.

3. Show some versatility in subject matter.
4. Include subjects you like best.
5. Include some black-and-white illustrations.

Secure the illustrations evenly in the portfolio, using small pieces of folded tape on the back of the four corners of the artwork. Snap out any pages of the portfolio that you do not need.

Art done on illustration board should not be left out if it is among your best. It can be slipped behind the plastic in your portfolio if it is not too heavy. Protect work on heavier board with an overlay, and carry it along with your portfolio.

The samples in your student portfolio should be replaced one by one with illustrations from jobs as you begin to work at your profession. Your goal is to replace all of the student efforts with professional artwork.

Finding Your Clients

Working as your own sales representative, you may have to visit many potential clients before finding freelance work. The contacts must also be renewed from time to time so that a client keeps you in mind for future work.

At the outset, who are your potential clients? Following is a list of clients who buy illustrations:

EDITORIAL ILLUSTRATION

1. Book designers
2. Book, magazine, and textbook publishing companies (contact the art director)
3. Advertising agencies (contact the art director)
4. Record companies (contact the art director)

PRODUCT ILLUSTRATION

1. Advertising agencies (contact the art director)
2. Retail stores

CHILDREN'S BOOK ILLUSTRATION

1. Book designers and design companies

2. Publishing companies for children's books and textbooks (contact the art director)

FASHION ILLUSTRATION

1. Retail clothing stores
2. Advertising agencies (contact the art director)
3. Clothes designers

BIOLOGICAL & MEDICAL ILLUSTRATION

1. Publishers of books, textbooks, and journals
2. Pharmaceutical companies
3. Medical colleges
4. Book designers
5. Hospitals
6. Manufacturers of surgical supplies and other medical materials

ARCHITECTURAL & MECHANICAL ILLUSTRATION

1. Architectural and engineering companies

2. Publishing companies (contact the art director)
3. Manufacturers

Firms like publishing companies and advertising agencies depend on art directors to review freelance portfolios. Some art directors have regular hours or days of the week set aside to review portfolios.

How can you find clients if you live outside a metropolitan area where there are no large publishing companies, designers, or agencies?

1. Make a trip into the closest large city and spend some time visiting potential clients. Once you have made contact, it is possible to work through the mail. Visit every six months to renew your contacts.
2. Mail slides of your artwork to publishers and agencies. Enclose a stamped, self-addressed envelope for the return of your slides.

Promoting Yourself

Consider making a self-promotional card or sample to leave behind with a client. Here is a list of examples from the least expensive to the most expensive:

1. Hand-printed cards with your name, address, and telephone number. Buy plain or colored cards, and hand print the information on each one. This takes a little extra time, but it is very inexpensive. It is efficient to have the information already printed so that you do not have to look for a pencil and paper to leave your phone number with a client. *Estimated cost = $1.*
2. "Instant Print" business cards. Instant printing is less expensive than metal-plate offset printing, but it will not reproduce shading or values. If you would like to include a sample of illustration on the card, pen-and-ink line artwork reproduces best. Lettering will reproduce well. Hand letter, use press type, or buy hot-press lettering with your name, address, and phone number typed on sticky-backed paper for about $4. *Estimated cost = $15.*
3. Business cards with one halftone illustration, name, address, and telephone number. A screen will reproduce shading and values on a card. *Estimated cost = $30.*
4. A sample page 8½″ × 11″ with one halftone illustration. An illustration with shading and values can be reproduced on the page, along with your name, address, and telephone number. *Estimated cost = $40.*
5. A sample page 8½″ × 11″ with reproductions of four illustrations. Four different illustrations are reproduced on the page, along with your name, address, and telephone number. *Estimated cost = $95.*
6. A sample page 8½″ × 11″ with reproductions of four illustrations, reproduced in full color, along with your name, address, and telephone number. *Estimated cost = $300.*

All of these except for #6 are reproduced in a single color, usually black, dark blue, or brown. The cost of printing in full color is so expensive that it is usually not worth the extra money. A good reproduction in black and white is usually sufficient.

The most effective card or sample sheet features examples of your best artwork. Color artwork can be reproduced in black and white if it has good contrast in the light and dark values. Large-sized artwork can be reduced to fit three or four examples on one page. Since a business card is small, you might consider reproducing a detail from an illustration instead of the entire picture. If you make a drawing specifically for the promotional piece, such as the business card, make it typical of your other artwork so that it will remind a client of your portfolio.

Choose a typeface that is simple, and either apply it yourself, as press-type, or have it typed for a small fee. The lettering should look simple, unobtrusive, and professional with no crooked or broken letters. Do not try to be too clever with the design and lettering. The artwork should stand out as most important, and the lettering should not detract from it.

All of the costs listed will vary according to your choice of paper, color of ink, cost of lettering, and whether your image bleeds off the paper. Paper is available in many different weights, textures, and colors. Very fine details will reproduce best on coated stock. Heavier paper is better for business cards. A colored ink will cost more than black ink. Although a printer will charge more if your image bleeds off the edge of the card or sample sheet, the cost may be worth it for a card, since it increases the image area. For a sample sheet it may make more sense to have a border around the illustration. All of these points can be discussed in more detail with a printer, who will answer your questions and give you a cost estimate for a job. If an estimate is too high, most printers will give you suggestions on how you can cut the cost.

Finding Your Style

There are many illustrators whose work is recognizable from their style and technique. You might wonder if you should be looking for a style of your own.

Let us define "style" as a personal way of using techniques and treating subject matter that sets you apart from other artists. An artist begins to find his or her own style by experimenting with several techniques and choosing among them to specialize in one. Different techniques and subject matter will attract artists with different personalities. The choices you make, consciously and unconsciously, will determine your style.

The more drawings and illustrations you make, the more your style will develop. Making several illustrations can be compared to looking at yourself in the mirror many times. Every time you look at

yourself, you discover something new about your appearance. In the same way, every illustration you make, whether you consider it a success or a failure, shows you something new about yourself. Look at each illustration and ask yourself if you are being bold, timid, cool, patient, impatient, controlled, experimental, or vague. The technique and subject matter in the illustration may reflect these and other qualities. Given time, you will include in your illustration only those qualities you prefer and you will be able to eliminate the others.

With time and energy, your style will become more personal and interesting. It is a developing and maturing process. Your style will evolve naturally as you work, beginning as a student and developing further as a professional.

Glossary

ACETATE—thin plastic sold in sheets or rolls, available clear or frosted; can be used to make overlays for illustrations.

ACRYLIC PAINTS—paint in which the vehicle is an acrylic resin. Acrylic paints can be diluted with water but are water-resistant once they dry. Available in tubes or jars in assorted colors.

AIR COMPRESSOR—machine that pumps compressed air, used for working an airbrush.

AIR GUN—See "airbrush."

AIRBRUSH—atomizer for applying a fine spray of paint or ink with compressed air. Fits comfortably in an artist's hand and is attached to an air compressor by an air hose.

ATTITUDE—arrangement or positioning of images that evokes a feeling or emotion.

BALANCE—visual stability produced by even distribution of weight on each side of a vertical or horizontal axis.

BLEED—illustration that runs off a page, so that the image is trimmed; image can also bleed into a border. An illustrator allows for bleed by increasing the size of an illustration by ½" on all sides that will bleed.

CARICATURE—drawing that captures a person's likeness by exaggerating and distorting characteristic features.

CLICHÉ—image that is overused; a stereotype.

COLD-PRESS PAPER—paper with a rough texture.

COLLAGE—composition of various materials or images glued on a picture surface.

COMPOSITION—the arrangement of images in an artistic form, with harmony among the relationships, balance, and proportion of images.

COMPREHENSIVE—preliminary drawing for an illustration that includes color.

CROSSHATCHING—technique of drawing with a series of parallel lines that cross each other obliquely.

CULTURAL SYMBOLISM—symbols that have meaning to people who share the same culture.

DECORATIVE—images that are pleasing for ornamental qualities.

DEEP SPACE—space that appears to have a three-dimensional quality, receding back into the picture plane.

DESIGN—to conceive or plan out in one's mind or on paper; the plan or conception of an illustration.

EDITORIAL ILLUSTRATIONS—illustrations that usually, but not always, accompany a story, article, or book. Illustrations in books, magazines, newspapers, and on record-album covers are considered editorial illustrations.

FANTASY—inventive design, weird or disordered image characterized by highly fanciful, supernatural elements.

FLAT SPACE—space in a drawing that appears two-dimensional.

FRISKET, LIQUID—liquid similar in appearance to rubber cement, which dries quickly into a waterproof surface. Can be applied to protect images from paint and later rubbed off.

FRISKET PAPER—paper used for stenciling when painting with an airbrush. The sticky side is protected by a sheet of waxed paper, which is peeled off at the time of use.

FROSTED ACETATE—popular material for

overlays; transparent and textured on one side so that it can be used as a drawing surface with pencils or pen-and-ink.

GESTURE—motion and attitude of an image as a means of expression.

GLAZING—painting technique using transparent paint to render images by applying successive layers. Each application is called a "glaze."

GRAPHITE PAPER—tissue paper coated on one side with graphite; used like carbon paper to duplicate an image.

HALFTONE—engraving made from an image photographed through a screen and then etched so that the details of the image are reproduced in dots.

HOT-PRESS PAPER—paper characterized by a smooth texture.

IMPRESSIONISTIC—in the manner of impressionism, a theory or practice of painting developed among French painters in the late 1800s, which depicts the natural appearances of objects with dabs or strokes of paint to simulate reflected light.

INK WASH—ink diluted with water.

LIGHT TABLE—table or transparent surface that has a light mounted under it. Paper becomes more transparent when set on a light table; used by illustrators to trace and make overlays easily.

MECHANICAL—type proofs and artwork positioned and mounted for photographic reproduction.

MECHANICAL CROSSHATCHING—crosshatching made with a straightedge tool such as a ruler (see Crosshatching).

MASK—to protect or cover; frisket paper is a "mask" for airbrushing.

MAT—border that frames a drawing in the standard technique for preparing artwork to hang on a wall.

MOUNT—to secure a drawing on a board.

OIL PAINTS—paints with an oil base; can be diluted with turpentine.

OPAQUE—ability to cover a surface. Opaque paint covers the paper or canvas it is painted on, as opposed to transparent paint, which allows the surface to show through.

OVERLAY—piece of paper or plastic mounted as a flap on top of an illustration. Overlays serve several functions. A protective overlay is always mounted on a finished illustration.

PAINTERLY—painting technique that does not try to hide or disguise brushstrokes. Brushstrokes or pen marks are vigorously applied with no effort to smooth out the texture.

PERSONAL SYMBOLISM—symbols that have meaning only for an individual and his or her close friends and family.

PICTORIAL—drawing with recognizable images.

PORTFOLIO—large notebook or folder containing samples of illustrations.

PORTRAIT—drawing or painting that captures the likeness of a person.

PRODUCT ILLUSTRATION—illustration of products, usually for the purpose of advertising.

REGISTER MARKS—corner marks placed on an illustration and its overlay to ensure that the colors of the two will meet perfectly when photographed.

ROUGH DRAWING—preliminary drawing for an illustration.

SCRATCHBOARD—specially prepared board with a chalk and black ink surface or white board with a chalk surface only.

SHADE—to draw or paint an image to create the effect of light and dark tone or shading. Also, a color produced by adding black to a first color.

STIPPLING—technique of making dots or flecks of paint or ink. A stippled drawing is made by using many small touches that together produce an even or softly graded shadow.

SURREALISM—artwork that is a distortion

or rearrangement of reality.

SYMBOLISM—images that express abstractions or ideas; the use of such images.

THUMBNAIL SKETCH—quick sketch to work out the design for an illsutration.

TONE—color quality or relative value; tint or shade of color.

TRANSPARENT—capable of being seen through. Transparent paint will allow the white of paper or canvas to show through.

UNIVERSAL SYMBOLS—symbols recognized throughout the world by people in many different cultures.

WASH—to paint a thin solution of paint or ink with a brush in a broad sweep.

X-ACTO KNIFE—metal handle that can hold blades of various sizes for cutting frisket paper, press-type, and trimming. A #11 blade is used for most illustration and design purposes.

Bibliography

History of Illustration

Bliss, Douglas Percy, *The History of Wood Engraving.* New York: Dutton, 1928.

Blum, Andre, *The Origins of Printing and Engraving.* New York: Scribner's, 1978.

Blumenthal, Joseph, *Art of the Printed Book, 1455-1955.* Boston: Godine, 1973.

Chibbett, D. G., *The History of Japanese Printing and Book Illustration.* Tokyo and New York: Kodansha, 1977.

Evans, Hilary, and Mary Evans, *Sources of Illustration: 1500-1900.* New York: Hastings House, 1972.

Hofer, Philip, *Baroque Book Illustration: A Short Survey.* Cambridge, MA: Harvard Univ. Press, 1970.

Reid, Forest, *Illustrators of the Eighteen Sixties: An Illustrated Survey of the Work of 58 Artists.* New York: Dover, 1975.

Sainton, Roger, *Art Nouveau Posters and Graphics.* New York: Rizzoli, 1977.

Wakeman, Geoffrey, *Victorian Book Illustration: The Technical Revolution.* Detroit: Gale Research, 1973.

Illustration Subjects

Bader, Barbara, *American Picture Books from Noah's Ark to The Beast Within.* New York: Macmillan, 1976.

Coulin, Claudius, *Step by Step Perspective Drawing for Architects, Draftsmen, and Designers.* New York: Van Nostrand, 1971.

Dember, Sol, *Complete Airbrush Techniques, for Commercial, Technical, and Industrial Applications.* Indianapolis: Bobbs-Merrill, 1974.

Doten and Boulard, *Costume Drawing.* New York: Grosset & Dunlap.

Freeman, Larry G., and Ruth Freeman, *The Child and His Picture Book.* Watkins Glen, NY; Century House, 1967.

Klemin, Diana, *Children's Illustrated Books.* New York: Potter, 1970.

Larkin, David, ed., *Once Upon a Time, Some Contemporary Illustrations of Fantasy.* New York: Peacock Press/Bantom, 1976.

McGinty, Tim, *Drawing Skills in Architecture.* Dubuque, 1A: Kendall-Hunt, 1980.

Maurello, S. Ralph, *The Complete Airbrush Book.* New York: Amiel, 1954.

Munce, Howard, *Magic and Other Realism.* New York: Hastings House, 1979.

Nakamura, Julia, and Massy Nakamura, *Your Future in Medical Illustrating, Art and Photography.* New York: Rosen Press, 1971.

Newberry and Caldecott Awards. Minneapolis: Univ. of Minnesota Press, 1966-1975.

Ridley, Pauline, *Fashion Illustration*. New York: Rizzoli, 1979.

Sloane, Eunice, *Illustrating Fashion*. New York: Harper, 1977.

Suares, Jean-Claude, *Art of the Times*. New York: Avon, 1973.

Vertes, Marcel, *Art and Fashion*. New York and London: Studio Publications, 1944.

Whalley, Joyce I., *Cobwebs to Catch Flies: Illustrated Books for the Nursery and Schoolroom*. Berkeley: Univ. of California Press, 1975.

White, Jan V., *Editing by Design: Word-&-Picture Communication for Editors and Designers*. New York: Bowker, 1974.

Wilson, Adrian, *The Design of Books*. Layton, Utah: Peregrine Smith, 1974.

Zweifel, Frances, *Handbook of Biological Illustrations*. Chicago: Univ. of Chicago Press, 1961.

General Skills

Klemin, Diana, *The Illustrated Book, Its Art and Craft*. New York: Potter, 1970.

Mendelowitz, Daniel M., *A Guide to Drawing*. New York: Holt, 1976.

A

Abstract expressionism, 6
Abstract symbols, 107–8
Acetate, 88, 89, 92
    defined, 165
Acrylics, 22, 60, 71–75
    airbrushing, 80
    with colored pencils, 67, 69–70
    defined, 165
    materials, 73
    with oil paints, 75–77
    painting techniques, 73–75
Advertising, 138–41
Agents, 160
Airbrush, 80–81
    defined, 165
    selecting, 81
Airbrushing, 71, 74, 78–87, 92
    airbrush, 80–81, 165
    characteristics, 78–79
    colored inks, 65
    getting ready, 81, 84
    techniques, 84–87
Air compressor, 81, 165
Allen, Julian, 123, 134
American folk art, 136
Analogous color scheme, 63–64
Architectural illustration, 155–57, 161–62
Artificial light, skin color in, 135
Attitude, defined, 165

B

Balance:
    composition and, 12, 15, 16
    defined, 165
Beardsley, Aubrey, 3, 4, 48
Bewick, Thomas, 3
Birren, Faber, 62
Black watercolor, 54, 56–57
Bleed, 21–22, 94
    defined, 165
Block books, 2
Boner, Ulrich, 2
Book of the Dead, The, 2
Breton, André, 119

Brown, Marcia, 149
Business cards, 162–63

C

Canvas:
    artwork on, care of, 94
    stretched, 71, 73, 75
Caricature, 136–38
    defined, 165
Carpenter, Mia, 147
Cartooning, 23, 109, 135
Cartridge pen, 36, 38
Chambers, Bill, 74
Children's books, 121, 127, 130, 148–50,
    161
China, 2
Chrome, drawing, 113
Clichés, 106
    defined, 165
Clients, finding, 161–62
Cold-press paper, 35, 165
Collage:
    composition, 124–26
    defined, 165
    technique, 29
Collier, John, 130, 131
Color guides, 89–90
Color Psychology & Color Therapy (Birren),
    62
Color separations, 87–93
    three- and four-color, 93
    two-color, 87–93
Color theory, 59–65
    basic colors, 60–61
    color associations, 62–63
    color schemes, 63–65
    color values, 61–62
    color wheel, 59–60, 62
    complementary colors, 61
    hue, 61
    intensity, 62
    warm and cool colors, 62
Color wheel, 59–60, 62
Colored inks, 65
Colored pencils, 19, 22, 67–70
    drawing techniques, 67–69
    with watercolors and acrylics, 69–70

Coloring book methods, 88–93
Colors:
　blending in airbrushing, 85
　complementary, 61
　drawing people in, 133–35
　primary, 60
　secondary, 60
　tertiary, 60–61
　warm and cool, 62
Communication Arts Color Guide for Offset
　　Lithography, 89
Complementary colors, 61
Complementary color scheme, 64–65
Composition, 12–17
　balance, 12, 15–16
　defined, 165
　interest, 16
　motion, 16
　symmetrical, 14, 15
Comprehensive drawing, 10, 22
　defined, 165
　pencil-acrylic method, 69–70
Conceptual art, 6, 7
Condak, Clifford, 58
Contoured crosshatching, 42–43
Copy camera, 93
Copy machine, reducing with, 28
Crayons, 92
Crosshatching, 36, 37, 40–43
　with colored pencils, 67
　contoured, 42–43
　defined, 165
　mechanical, 40, 42
　overlay for, 92
　on scratchboard, 47
Cubism, 4
Cultural images, 99, 106
Cultural symbolism, 165

D

Dada, 7
Dali, Salvador, 119, 124
Dance of Death, 2
Deep space, defined, 165
Denis, Maurice, 3
DesCombes, Roland, 39
Design, defined, 165
Designer, role of, 29
Diamond Sutra, 2
Difficult subjects, drawing, 109–15
Dip pen, 36, 38
Drafting, 152, 155
Drawing:
　from life, 23–24

　from memory, 22–23
　from photographs, 24–29
Drop shadow, 153
Dürer, Albrecht, 2

E

Edelstein, Der (Boner), 2
Editorial illustration, 161
　defined, 165
Egypt, 2
Emotions:
　advertising and, 140–41
　communicating, 102–3, 105
　of figures, 133
Engraving, 3
Etching, 3
Etching needle, 47
Europe, 2
Expressionism, 4, 6

F

Fantasy illustration, 6, 7, 101–2, 118–26,
　　143, 147
　collage composition, 124–26
　defined, 165
Fashion illustration, 144–48, 161
Fasolino, Teresa, 70, 71
Figure drawing, 127–33
Flat space, defined, 165
Flesh, painting, 133–35
Format, 152
Four-color separation, 93
Freelance illustration, 160–63
　clients, 161–62
　portfolio preparation, 160–61
　self-promotion, 162–63
Frisket:
　liquid, 53, 56, 57–58, 165
　paper, 54, 84, 87, 165
Frosted acetate, 92, 165–66
Funk art, 6

G

Gesso, 73, 75
Gesture, defined, 166
Gist, Linda, 54

Glass, drawing, 112–13
Glazing technique:
    acrylics, 74–75
    defined, 166
    colored pencils, 69
Gouache, 57, 67
Graphite paper, 35, 56, 67, 73, 77, 125, 137
    defined, 166
    tracing with, 27–28
    use with scratchboard, 47
Grove, David, 129, 139

H

Hair, painting, 135
Halftone photography, 34, 57, 92
    defined, 166
Hand printing, 3
Holbein, Hans the Younger, 2
Holland, Brad, 42, 43, 116, 118, 119, 122, 123, 132, 133
Homer, Winslow, 4
Hot-press paper, 35, 166
Hue, 61

I

Illustration board, 52, 54, 71, 73, 92, 161
    care of artwork on, 94
    selecting, 35
Images, 99–106
    ambiguity, avoiding, 105–6
    communicating essence, 108–9
    in fantasy illustration, 121, 125
    gesture and attitudes of, 102–5
    relationship of, 100–102
Impressionism, 4, 6, 166
Ink wash, 52–53, 92, 166
Inks:
    airbrushing, 80
    colored, 65
    for dip and cartridge pens, 36, 38
    similarity to black watercolor, 56
    wash, 52, 53, 92
Intaglio printing, 3
Interpretive subjects, 10

J

Johnson, Doug, 82, 83, 86, 138, 139

L

Leech, Richard, 78, 79, 114, 139, 140
Light table, 27, 35, 67, 88, 166
Line illustration, 34–48
    crosshatching, 36, 37, 40–43
    ink wash and, 52, 53
    materials, 35
    methods, 35–36
    overlay for, 92
    pens, 36, 38
    scratchboard, 45–48
    stippling, 43
    zip-a-tone, 45
Linseed oil, 76, 77
Lithography, 3
Lobel, Arnold, 148, 149
Luci, 26

M

McLean, Wilson, 72
Magazines, collecting, 26
Masks, wearing when airbrushing, 83–84, 166
Masonite, 71, 73, 76
Mats, 94, 166
Mechanical, defined, 166
Mechanical crosshatching, 40, 42, 69, 166
Mechanical illustration, 155–57, 161–62
Medical illustration, 154–55, 161
Memory, drawing from, 22–23
Metals, shiny, drawing, 113
Minimal art, 6
Monochromatic color scheme, 63
Mood, 103, 107, 108, 121
    in product illustration, 143
Morris, William, 3
Mounting, 94, 166

O

Oil paints, 75–77, 166
    with acrylics, 75–77
    care of finished work, 94
    materials, 75–77
Olson, Judy, 30
Opaque paint, 166
Otnes, Fred, 96, 125
Overlay, 88, 89, 91–93, 152, 166
    ink wash and, 52
    materials for, 92

P

Painterly style, 29
    defined, 166
Painting, 2, 6, 28
    acrylics, 22, 60, 67, 69–70, 71–75, 76,
        77, 80
    flesh, 133–35
    oil paints, 75–77
    tempera, 67
    watercolors, 19, 22, 34, 54–59, 65, 67,
        69, 80, 92
Paper, selecting, 35
Parrish, Maxfield, 6, 26
Pattern painting, 6
Pen and ink, 34–35, 116, 118, 119
    overlay for, 92
    See also Line illustration
Pencils, 92
    colored, 69–70
Penny Magazine, 3
People, drawing, 127–38
    caricature, 136–38
    in color, 133–35
    portraits, 135–36
Persistence of Memory, The (Dali), 119
Personal symbolism, 166
Perspective, 14, 15, 17
Peterson, Lawrence, 153
Pettinari, James, 156, 157
Pfister, Albrecht, 2
Photoengraving, 3
Photographic four-color separation, 93
Photographs/photography, 6, 7
    drawing from, 24–29
    effect on art, 28–29
    introduction as illustration, 3
    in medical illustration, 154
    product illustration and, 141
    use for rough drawings, 24–29
Photorealism, 6, 7, 28, 145, 146
Picasso, Pablo, 4
Pictorial drawing, 166
Pop art, 6
Portfolio:
    defined, 166
    preparing, 160–61
Portraits, 127, 128, 130, 132, 133, 135–38
    caricatures, 136–38
    defined, 166
Pratchenko, Paul, 144
Press-type, 152
Primary colors, 60
Product illustration, 138–44, 161, 166
    interpretive, 143–44
    realistic, 141–43

Projecting techniques, 26–28
Proportional scale wheel, 21

R

Realism, 7
    fantasy illustration and, 124
Red film, 88, 89, 92
Reducing, 20–21, 28, 35
Register marks, 166
Renaissance, 2
Representational art, 4, 6
Rockwell, Norman, 6
Rough drawing, 10, 19–29
    defined, 166
    drawing from life, 23–24
    drawing from memory, 22–23
    drawing from photographs, 24–29
    materials, 19, 22
    size, 20–22
    technique, 22
    transferring, 56, 67, 77
Ruby-red film, 88, 89, 92

S

Scratchboard, 45–48
    board, 45–46
    defined, 166
    techniques, 47–48
    tools, 46–47
Scribbling, 43
Secondary colors, 60
Shade, 61, 166
Shiny metals, drawing, 113
Silhouette, 22
    in half-tone photography, 92
Silverman, Burt, 34, 128, 131, 134, 137
Skin, painting, 133–35
Slides, tracing from, 26–27, 67, 73, 77, 125
Sorel, Edward, 44, 45, 104, 137
Stavrinov, George, 107, 145, 146
Steiner, Robert, 40, 41, 100, 101, 119, 120
Stencils, movable, 85–86
Stippling, 29, 43, 69
    defined, 166
Straightforward subject, 10
Style, 163
Subjects, straightforward v. interpretive, 10
Surrealism, 6, 7, 119–20
    defined, 166–67

Surreal illustration, 101–2, 118–21, 147
Symbolism, 98–100, 102
    abstract, 107–8
    defined, 167
    personal, 166
    in portraits, 136
    in product illustration, 140
    universal, 167
    See also Images
Symmetrical composition, 14, 15

T

Technical illustration, 151–53
Tempera paints, 67
Templates, 152
Tenniel, John, 149
Tertiary colors, 60–61
Textures, 39, 43, 45, 69
    airbrushing over, 86
Thoma, Marta, 12, 32, 34, 40–42, 50, 55,
    66, 68, 69, 75, 76, 82, 90, 91, 98,
    101, 120, 123, 136, 137
Thoman, Kim, 72
Three-color separation, 93
Thumbnail sketch, 10, 11–16, 23, 167
    composition, 12–16
    ideas, 11–12
    materials, 11
Tints, 61
Tone:
    airbrushing, 85
    defined, 167
    inkwash, 52, 53
Toothbrush spraying, 54
Topographic illustration, 157
Toulouse-Lautrec, 4
Tracing techniques, 26–28
Transparent paint, 167
Turpentine, 76, 77
Two-color illustration, 87–93
    coloring book methods, 88–92
    integrated, 92–93

U

Universal symbols, 167

V

Value:
    color, 61–62
    crosshatching and, 39, 40, 42
    patterns and, 43, 45
Varnish, 76, 94
Vellum, 92

W

Warhol, Andy, 6
Wash, defined, 167
Water, drawing, 109–12
Watercolor board, 54, 56
Watercolor paper, 52, 54
    stretching, 55
Watercolors, 19, 22, 34, 54–59, 92
    airbrushing, 80
    black watercolor technique, 56–57
    with colored inks, 65
    with colored pencils, 67, 69
    full spectrum, 57–59
    stretching paper, 55
    transfer of rough drawing, 56
Wolfe, Bruce, 110, 142, 143
Wong-Ligda, Edward, 70
Wood block printing, 2, 3

X

X-acto knife, 45, 46, 55, 83, 84, 87, 89,
    167

Z

Zip-a-tone, 45, 152

DATE DUE			
DEC 1 2	DEC 2 0		
FEB 2 3 1994	DEC 1 1 '92		
APR 6 1994			
OCT 0 4 1994	JUL 2 9 1999		
OCT 1 8	MAR 2 4 2000		
SEP 2 3 1985			
OCT 8 1985	FEB 1 1 2001		
	DEC 0 5		
APR 8 '87	APR 2 5 2006		
SEP 9 '86			
OCT			
DEC 3 1 '88